SCHOOLING 1963–1970

By the same author

TECHNICAL EDUCATION FOR ADOLESCENTS

SCHOOLING
1963–1970

———

C. H. DOBINSON, M.A., B.Sc.
Professor of Education, University of Reading

GEORGE G. HARRAP & CO. LTD
London Toronto Wellington Sydney

First published in Great Britain 1963
by GEORGE G. HARRAP *&* CO. LTD
182 High Holborn, London, W.C.1

© *C. H. Dobinson 1963*

Composed in Times New Roman type and printed by
William Clowes and Sons, Limited, London and Beccles
Made in Great Britain

Preface

THERE has been widespread recognition for many years, especially since 1945, that much of English education needs to change to meet the changed conditions of life.

Discontents are continually expressed with various aspects and levels of the system and with the studies themselves, and suggestions for modification are put forward from many quarters.

This book attempts to bring together a number of the important criticisms of recent years, and some of the proposals for improvement, and to give them a certain degree of unity.

There is little new in it; but my motive for writing is a desire to stimulate discussion so that something might be done quickly for a major reorganization of English education.

Contents

CHAPTER ONE

What's Wrong: Schools and the Social Environment

THERE have been many statements of the aims of education and there will be many more. It seems doubtful, however, if a more constructive one will ever be found than that which Sir Herbert Read resurrected for us from the writings of William Godwin in his *Enquirer* (1797):

> The true object of education, like that of every other moral process, is the generation of happiness.

The writer would wish to emphasize the word *generation* in this statement, because the phrase 'the pursuit of happiness', enshrined in the Declaration of Independence and familiar to hundreds of millions of people, has not quite the same meaning, though both have elements in common. As for a definition of happiness, each reader must apply his own, perhaps with the help of the philosophers both modern and ancient.

But if we are prepared to take Godwin's dictum as a starting point, then it is clear that we are at once concerned not so much with the classroom as with the social environment, for this is where happiness must mainly be generated. Moreover, since education, in its greatest dosage, is always given to the young, it is the social environment of twenty years on, rather than that of today, which should be the chief concern of the educator.

Education and the social environment

Yet, by and large, education has never given as much attention even to the *existing* social environment as it has to the social environment of the past. As late as 1942 Professor E. H. Carr in his classic *Conditions of Peace* could write: 'Learning commonly lags at least a generation behind life.' Indeed many, perhaps most, educators have seen their responsibility as mainly that of handing down the heritage of past traditions, ideas and symbols, of discouraging any critical evaluation of these, and of maintaining, as far as might be, a stable set of values in the religious, political and economic fields of thought. This statement holds true not only for those countries where a regular 'priesthood' of professional educators has long existed, but also for primitive societies, where the training of the young is the responsibility of all, and where professional educators are a luxury not even sought after.

Indeed, it is possible that the malaise found among adolescents of many countries today is partly the result of the backward looking education which they receive from their school teachers. To the adolescent his teachers usually represent everything that is orthodox and they seem clearly to be strong supporters of the Establishment, in whatever form it exists in their particular country. Few teachers can be identified with protest marchers or with any kind of reform group, or are known to say to their adolescent classes: 'The challenge that faces us all today, both you and me, is to change. . . .' No, alas, teachers as a rule, especially in the United Kingdom and even more in the United States, are identified with the *status quo* rather than with any form of change. Arnold Toynbee in 1947 can write:

> We have to abolish War and Class—and abolish them now—under pain, if we flinch or fail, of seeing them win a victory over man which, this time, would be conclusive and definitive.[1]

And Canon Evans, the Chancellor of Southwark Cathedral, fifteen years later:

> Ours is still one of the most acutely divided societies in the world, notwithstanding whatever advance we have made in our social services,

and

Big differences in income exist between workers in different industries, but these are as nothing to the difference of income between any manual worker and those who use money as the one tool of their trade.[2]

But inflammatory words of this kind, which might link together in common enterprise of thought angry young men and teacher—if the teacher were to quote such words and then discuss their implications—are seldom heard in our classrooms. For they might seem an attempt to sabotage the Combined Cadet Force of our Grammar and Public Schools, or to favour socialism, even if they are the considered judgements of don and prelate.

No, in general, schools in England and Wales today, and in many other countries, are not really interested in the social and economic environment of the future and in the generation of happiness. Whilst they set out, as a by-product of their work, unobtrusively to establish conformism to certain codes of thought and habits of behaviour, they are primarily concerned with the ingestion and written regurgitation of information, and despite the resistance of a minority of teachers, almost every influence exerted upon them tends to keep them so.

In this respect schools have changed so little in a century that some of Herbert Spencer's strictures about English education in 1859 seemed, in 1959, as though they were contemporary criticism:

Examinations being once passed, books are laid aside; the greater part of what has been acquired, being unorganized, soon drops out of recollection; what remains is mostly inert—the art of applying knowledge not having been cultivated; and there is but little power either of accurate observation or independent thinking.[3]

Education and world harmony

Similarly, if we survey broadly the history of education in Europe during the last two centuries we can see how, with a few exceptions such as the Ecoles Centrales founded by the Revolutionaries in France in 1792, education has continually failed to respond to the changing needs of either society or of the human race.

Or, again, having regard to the attempts to establish, after World War I, a community of nations, could we really regard the school curriculum of almost any nation, as it existed between 1919 and 1933, as having any relation whatsoever to the ideals and purposes of humanity as expressed through the mouths of statesmen and preachers? After Hitler's advent to power in March 1933, German education, which from Fichte in 1802 till 1918 had been deliberately used as an instrument of nationalism, became the principal means of preparing for the Nazi conquest of Europe. Between the two World Wars perhaps only in England, in Scandinavia and to a lesser extent in the U.S.A., was any progress made in reducing nationalistic self-glorification in and through the schools. Looking back over the educational failures of the years from 1919 to 1933, and forward through the overhanging clouds of nuclear fallout, we may feel disposed, with St. Paul, to say:

> And the times of this ignorance God winked at; but now commandeth all men everywhere to repent because he hath appointed a day in which he will judge the world. . . .[4]

The over-all failure of education to measure up to its responsibilities was of relatively little importance at times when the rate of change of social and economic life was fairly slow. But now that the tempo of change is so great that even many of the intelligentsia of the most advanced nations find it hard to adjust their outlook with sufficient rapidity to keep it both equable and constructive, the retrospective fixation of education must be ended.

Unfortunately, too few realize that this can only be achieved by a fresh re-statement of objectives and these, as Godwin's statement makes plain, must be defined in relation to the political economic and social environment that lies a whole generation ahead.

It is vain to declare that we cannot visualize this. Of course, in its details the future is inevitably obscure or it would not be the future. But its general outlines have been sufficiently clear for at least two nations, Sweden and France, to base, with outstanding success, their social, educational and economic developments on plans looking twenty years ahead. One thesis of this book is that, unless many nations, and especially we of the United Kingdom, are prepared to adjust, much more rapidly than we are at present doing, our education to the changes needed in society, then wonderful opportunities for the improvement of human life all over the world will be thrown away.

It is difficult, we have admitted, to see more than the general outline of what could and should lie twenty years ahead. But it can surely be safely affirmed that, unless the world is well-nigh destroyed by nuclear war:

(a) enough food can be produced to feed all the mouths in the world;

(b) there will be adequate leisure, at least in the countries which are already economically advanced, for all men and women to be, in the words of Condorcet: 'Strangers to none of the high and delicate feelings which honour human nature'[5];

(c) there will be adequate resources of energy for the abolition of those forms of physical labour and industrial life which are seriously harmful to the human body;

(d) the peaceful and happy existence of communities will call for wider individual participation in the responsibilities of industry and commerce and also in local and central government;

(e) the rate of change will be so fast that neither in terms of his vocation, nor in terms of his contribution to community life, will a citizen be able to keep abreast of events without continual learning and self-adjustment.

In other words, life and learning will be universally recognized as synonymous and mutually dependent. Admittedly these paragraphs are reminiscential of what Condorcet wrote, with prophetic accuracy, just before his death in 1792, but they are none the worse for that; indeed, they benefit from keeping such good company:

> New machines will add to man's strength and improve at once the quality and accuracy of his productions and will diminish the time and labour that has to be expended on them.
>
> Accidents in factories will be foreseen and prevented and unhealthy conditions due either to the work itself or to the climate will be eliminated . . . not only will the same amount of ground support more people, but everyone will produce more, will satisfy his wants more fully and have less work to do. . . .
>
> Nations will invite foreigners to share equally in all the benefits men enjoy either through the bounty of nature, or by their own industry.[6]

In short, it is clear that, within twenty years, if humanity uses aright its opportunities, in the economically advanced countries the situation of every citizen will be comparable with that of a Free Man in Athens at the time of Plato. With approximately four slaves to minister, directly or indirectly, to the needs of every free man, woman and child, the life of such a person was in those days concerned mainly with the development and utilization of those gifts and qualities which, in the animal kingdom, are the prerogative of man alone. In the post-Platonic period, according to Marrou, men and women took pride in their personal culture:

> That is why we find on so many burial monuments an account of the intellectual culture of the deceased. Whether these records are due to their expressed wish or to the initiative of their descendants, they are shown to us as men of letters, orators, philosophers, lovers of art, as women musicians and so on.
>
> These monuments do not necessarily belong, as had been previously supposed, to professional intellectuals such as writers, artists, lecturers, and teachers; we know today that they were dedicated to people whose work lay in entirely different fields; these people were doctors, officials of various kinds, merchants and so on; but, whatever they were, all had wished only one thing to be recorded on their tomb; that they were people who had been initiated into the learning of the Muses, that they had access to this incomparable treasure, the culture of the mind and of the soul.[7]

It is here apposite to recall Matthew Arnold's famous definition of culture as 'the acquainting ourselves with the best that has been known and said in the world, and thus with the history of the human spirit'.

The changes in the nature of work

Even today the happy situation in which all in this country can have access to what is finest in art, music, literature and science is almost within grasp; yet automation has hardly begun to make its impact. Only in the autumn of 1962 was the first automatic, hot-steel, strip mill opened in the United Kingdom—in South Wales. Whilst we can take pride in the claim that this is also the first of its kind in the world, we know that it is only the forerunner of many and will lead to great reduction of demand in labour. Indeed we know that most of the skills based upon empiricism and upon the human senses are going to disappear except in the field of art.

In French educational planning the following approximate figures are given for distribution of workers by category in 1960:

(1) Technologists and managerial staff   5%
(2) Middle group: highly skilled technicians or the equivalent in Commerce   35%
(3) Manual workers, including skilled, semi-skilled and unskilled   60%

For 1970 it is estimated that the distribution will be:

(1) Technologists and managerial staff   25%
(2) Middle group: highly skilled technicians or the equivalent in Commerce   55%
(3) Manual workers, including skilled, semi-skilled and unskilled   20% [8]

In the U.S.A., in July 1962, a report was issued in the California Labour Statistics Bulletin showing that in ten years the ratio of production workers to the total in manufacturing employment had fallen from 76 per cent to 65 per cent. This was given as evidence of the growing effect of automation.[9]

When we look at this ever-increasing demand for people to fill positions at the creative, administrative and executive levels, the question that arises in our minds is—can we find a sufficient number of intelligent youngsters to train to fill these posts?

Have we the human resources to meet the challenge of upgrading?

This is a question often upon the lips of men holding responsible positions in industry, commerce and political life. Clearly, it is a question of absolutely fundamental importance for all planners and therefore we must here give it very careful consideration and attempt to find the answer.

First we should consider the facts of post-school human development. Everyone can give examples of persons who had little success at school but whose contribution to life through industry, commerce, agriculture, local government, church or literature has been very worthy. And there are outstanding examples, that readily come to mind, of really great men in all fields of life whose school records were very undistinguished. For example, Charles Darwin, speaking of his boyhood said:

> When I left school I was for my age neither high nor low in it; and I believe that I was considered by all my masters and by my father as a very ordinary boy, rather below the common standard in intellect.

Such cases put us on our guard against those who assure us, as some university dons continually do, that they have 'scraped the barrel' so far as talent for Higher Education is concerned.

Secondly, we now know, thanks largely to the Russians, that environment plays a very much larger share in the development of the child than we used to think. The old Adam in us all, expressed in pride of achievement, associates success with inherent qualities which we like to think we transmitted to our fortunate offspring, rather than to the advantages of home environment and better and longer schooling which we were able to provide for them.

As the late Lord Dewar aptly expressed this outlook:

'Every man believes in heredity till the son makes a fool of himself.' We should be better, not only individually, but in our social planning, if we frequently recited to ourselves the words of the Rev. Robert Herrick:

> What man is there can ever hope to swim
> If friend or fortune do not favour him?

The effects of primary schooling

At all events, we now *know* that an unfortunate home environment in nursery years, illness, poverty, family bereavement and distress, all these things and others, can as surely blight a life as a late frost in the spring can damage a bud and so mar the flower.

As for what happens in the early years of schooling, this, too, is something which in the past we have under-estimated. Indeed, we have hardly begun to record the effect of skilled handling in the primary school upon subsequent intellectual and personal development of the child. No one would deliberately subject a child to a mediocre teacher for experimental purposes, but if the subsequent development of comparable groups of children who have been handled by very able teachers and by average teachers could be recorded, we might get some evidence. Such investigations would need to be carried out in North America, Sweden or Norway as in most parts of this country the primary school teacher still has to give undue attention to the subjects of the 11 + examination, rather than encourage the development of the full spectrum of the child's abilities. But we might well find that the good teacher of small children makes a far greater difference to their subsequent careers than is generally recognized. For, as all who have observed fine teaching in primary schools can bear witness, this gives to the little ones that happiness and confidence which leads to self-expression and to an out-pouring of their embryonic powers in a wide range of creative activities.

The reverse situation arises when insensitive or ill-tempered reactions towards small children make learning unpalatable

2

and dries up many of the wells of interest.Whilst it is unlikely that anything will hold back the brilliant child, for the majority of children, clustered round the mean of intelligence distribution, it is likely to be an important factor of differentiation whether, or not, in the primary school, they come into the class of a very good teacher. All of which goes to show that by improving the quality of the teaching in our primary schools (which, as we shall show, depends largely on reducing the size of classes), we are likely to increase the proportion of the population who will subsequently be suited for the middle and upper parts of industry and commerce.

The effects of secondary schooling upon the adolescent

Of course, the story does not end there. Whilst today we do not, with Rousseau, regard adolescence as a stage of being born again:

> We are born so to speak twice over; born into existence, and born into life; born a human being, and born a man.[10]

we recognize that skilful handling by the teacher of this 'lion in a fever' and lessons of high quality and inspiration are of supreme importance at the adolescent stage. There are tens of thousands of people occupying positions of some importance who gladly and continually acknowledge, to themselves and to others, the inestimable debt they owe to a teacher or teachers under whose influence they came during adolescence, or whose lessons set their minds on fire and so determined the whole subsequent nature of their lives.

In view of his contribution to the welfare of humanity, perhaps the tribute of Pasteur to some of the men who taught him in his student days is the most outstanding. He called them *allumeurs d'âme* and regarded himself as one of their disciples.

CHAPTER TWO

What's Wrong: The Bottom Stream in Secondary Education

Selection for secondary education

WHILE relatively few parents feel much concern regarding the education of their children in the primary schools, most parents in England and Wales are deeply concerned about the secondary education of their offspring, because this is generally the decisive factor regarding the types of work which the youngsters will take up.

Because of the way in which secondary education was extended in this country, and in spite of the development of Comprehensive and Bilateral schools and the Comprehensive Junior High Schools of Leicestershire, we are still, for the majority of children, making important educational decisions when they are only eleven years of age. And the instruments which are used to classify the children are mainly standardized tests of 'intelligence', supplemented by carefully assessed achievement tests (often standardized as well) and by the subjective assessments of teachers. It is important to consider the assumptions which underlie these procedures. One of the first is that these enable us to identify what the Americans call 'the gifted child'. Fortunately, some extremely extensive psychological research, supported by funds from the U.S. Office of Naval Research and the U.S. Office of Education, has recently been brought to fruition by a team of workers under Professor J. P. Guilford of the University of Southern California. This was an investigation into the whole business of categories of talent and measuring them. Already the researches have established fifty-five different primary abilities and there are probably many more.

This has confirmed what thousands of teachers have long been saying, like Galileo under their breath, namely that 'the human mind is far more complex than can be inferred from present-day methods of identifying "the gifted" and, in particular, that traditional measures of I.Q. tap only a few of man's thinking abilities'. Indeed, the same writer[1] affirms:

> If present methods of identifying talent had been applied they would have eliminated many of the great men of the past.

What is more, if we are concerned to look for and encourage creative abilities, we must not, as in the past and present, concentrate on the groups that respond best to the school situation and its ethos. This is how Professor Guilford puts the matter:

> And which children should be regarded as gifted? The current answer, at least in many places, is the student with a high I.Q. and with high grades (the two indicators usually strongly correlated). Such children may be those who please their teachers most because they learn more rapidly under conditions that call for uniformity of thinking and acting within a group. The more creative child, who may be higher in divergent thinking abilities and not so high in cognitive abilities emphasized in present tests and examinations, may be a source of annoyance and not recognized as gifted. And how many children who are potential composers or artists, who are very high in concrete intelligence but not so high in academic intelligence, are missed when the 'gifted child' is selected.[2]

Such considerations, based on extensive research, and fitting in with human experience over the centuries, cannot be brushed aside. The educational planners of England and Wales have now to be brought to accept the fact that the whole business of selection of the gifted child is based on false assumptions and is resulting in a vast waste of creative ability and in the frustration of the lives of tens of thousands.

This is part of the answer we can give to those who say they are scraping the barrel.

Disappointment in secondary education

Whilst many, as we have pointed out, acknowledge with deep gratitude how much they owe to their secondary schooling, there are hundreds of thousands of disgruntled, unsuccessful people who are thus unsuccessful largely because they were bored at school and insisted on leaving school at the earliest possible moment. It is inevitable, because of the secondary school selection system of England and Wales, that the majority of these were 'unselected' children, such as, in most areas, are sent to Secondary Modern Schools.

So the remarks quoted below, all of them from pupils in Secondary Modern Schools, are important, because they throw light upon the way in which these pupils reacted to their studies:

> A girl: 'You get tired of sitting and doing nothing and just listening to the teacher talking. I only like the things we *do* ourselves. . . . I only like needlework and craft and cookery and we don't get enough of those, so I'll be glad to leave. I don't like the other lessons, Geography for one. Or History.'
>
> Another girl: 'I don't like school. I'm fed up with it. I don't like science to begin with. About plants and how they breathe. I'm not interested in that! *I'm not interested in how plants breathe.* I don't care *how* they do it. . . . I've had enough school.'
>
> A boy: 'I've had enough school. I want to do something—make a start at what I *really* want to do . . . I don't like French. I'm nearly top in it, but I don't like it. It's *boring*. I like woodwork, metalwork, art, electricity—where *you* do things. I'm not a good writer. I don't like writing, I like doing practical things, so I won't miss lessons. . . .'[3]

Lest anyone should say that these opinions are not typical, and that the majority of youngsters in Secondary Modern Schools do *not* leave at the earliest moment, let us quote from a letter of Professor D. V. Glass, of the London School of Economics, to *The Listener* of August 9th, 1962. Disagreeing with some views which had been expressed in a broadcast by Lord James, Vice-Chancellor of the University of York, Professor Glass called attention to the long-term study carried out by his colleague Dr. J. W. B. Douglas and others on the development of some 5,000 children from different parts of the country, and from all classes, all of whom were born in the first week of March 1946[4] and therefore had reached school-leaving age in 1961. Follow-up had shown that of the children who were in Secondary Modern Schools, 83 per cent had left immediately after their fifteenth birthday. By contrast, of the children of the same group attending Comprehensive and Multilateral Schools, only 44 per cent had left immediately upon reaching the age of 15.

This figure of 83 per cent, of a random sample of 5,000 Secondary Modern School pupils from all over the country, leaving school at the earliest possible moment cannot be evaded. Since the figure for immediate leavers from Comprehensive Schools is much lower, much of the fault clearly lies with the tripartite system. But even the figure for Comprehensive Schools (44 per cent becoming 'immediate leavers'), is really, if we will face it, a pretty ruthless commentary on the quality of the teaching and/or upon what seems to the youngsters its irrelevance to their lives.

The schools were made for the children, not the children for the schools. It is all in vain for teachers to endeavour to excuse themselves by such remarks as: 'This type of child isn't interested in things of the mind.' 'These youngsters couldn't care less about anything.' 'They don't want to learn: all they want to do is to play the fool.' Such excuses are the final condemnation of the teacher himself and conclusive evidence of his professional incompetence. The teacher's function is to create interests for the youngsters, to inspire them to care by 'getting under their skins' and relating school to the things they *do* care about and then gradually connecting these sentiments to others which are wider or more worthy.

The importance of day release

If enough teachers of the right quality and right training (for this is clearly at fault to a large measure) cannot be found at present, it is far better for these adolescents in Secondary

Modern Schools to escape at the age of 15 from the clutches of the mock-academics who are feeding them with a milk and water version of the Grammar School syllabuses, and go out to work.

But they should then have compulsory day release for education based on the Kerschensteiner principle that the daily work should be the central point from which all the studies radiate. Thus girls employed in florists' shops in Zurich learn, in their day-release school, to paint, draw and model flowers, to arrange them, to calculate costs of bouquets and wreaths and to make shop notices in attractive lettering. They learn from which parts of Switzerland or abroad the different flowers come, something about their cultivation and their history as cultivated plants, about species and genera, something about floral customs in other countries and so on. Of course, they have their civic studies too and of course they are, incidentally, all the time improving their ability to read, write and calculate. But they cannot, at any stage, say 'this study is of no relevance to my life'. So work and day release, especially since the latter will keep the young person under guidance until the age of 18, seems infinitely preferable to extending for another year a form of education which, as Professor Glass's figures show, is an utter failure with four young people out of five in Secondary Modern Schools saying, in effect, 'I've had enough of school.'

As long ago as 1938 the Spens Report[5] stressed the value of the vocational element in education and pointed to the remarkable success of Junior Technical Schools:

> We have found in the schools we visited an atmosphere of vitality, keenness and happiness that was not only refreshing, but afforded a sure index that the curriculum and its methods of treatment so appealed to the pupils that the process of education was developing smoothly and unrestrainedly.

In 1959 Major-General Cyril Lloyd, addressing the annual conference of the British Association for Commercial and Industrial Education on the topic 'Education and Training for

1965', stated that there were, in his view, five broad principles upon which we must work for the future. These were:

(1) The establishment of machinery for more precise identification of industrial needs with regard to vocational education.
(2) The development of general education along lines which are relevant to the modern world and not relevant to a world which has passed away.
(3) Proper integration of general education with vocational training.
(4) The introduction into education of the elementary facts of life in the economic and political sphere.
(5) The inclusion in education of physical activities, including skills, designed to develop the whole person.[6]

The Certificate of Secondary Education

Unfortunately, since 1959, things have not moved in those directions at all. As an attempt to provide motivation inside Secondary Modern Schools for the typical school-book studies, teachers have been organizing for some years, with a laudable fluidity, examinations which they conducted under arrangements approved by the Local Education Authority and which would award a Secondary School Certificate for satisfactory results. Unfortunately this movement gradually carried the majority of teachers in Secondary Modern Schools back into the old groove of written examinations based on standardized syllabuses applied over large areas. Soon, instead of being provided with an education which is both relevant to the modern world and relevant to the individual vocational needs of individual children, the majority of pupils of Secondary Modern Schools must be crammed—driven through the narrow gates provided by the Examiners.

The sort of effect that this seeking of the Secondary School Certificate is already having is well shown by the following unsolicited letter from a teacher in Devonshire:

As a teacher in a Secondary Modern School I am becoming increasingly depressed at the speed with which we are accepting the shackles of external examinations in their present form. Gone are the days when, if the class and I became absorbed in a subject which arose from the lesson, we could pursue it for as long as we wished. Now, too, we are tied by a syllabus and certain things have to be got through, however useless and irrelevant they may seem. Present examinations seem to me to be nothing but a memory test. Surely it's reasoning, initiative, adaptability and resourcefulness that are important. I suppose it is difficult to devise an examination that tests these qualities. It is certainly easier to teach to a syllabus, to just dish out the usual dreary material and not question its value, but it is not education. Yet now there is this fever for 'certificates' one can't, in fairness to the children, ignore them and it is only fair that our brighter children should have the same opportunities as the Grammar School children—so here we are in a web of our own making. People clamour for education but what is its value in its present form?

I am also concerned about the children with little academic ability. In a Secondary Modern School there are a fair number. If too much stress is placed on examinations and certificates they become even more convinced that they are inferior and this breeds hostility and resentment and an anti-social attitude. Yet many of these children work hard, although they achieve little. They are conscientious and painstaking and will make admirable employees if the employers can overcome their 'lack of certificate' phobia.

I feel that 'education' is not really meeting the needs of the younger generation. All it is providing is a certificate saying that they remember which is the prevailing wind in India, what is Boyle's Law, which King lived when—but they need to be able to question the treatment of events in the Daily Press, to distinguish 'slanted' writing from objective reporting, to enjoy good plays and films, to know about people in other countries and their present difficulties, to have some understanding of the economics of running a country—to know what sort of behaviour is responsible and what is not—I could go on for pages. Yet this sort of discussion has to be sandwiched in in odd moments—it won't get them through 'School Certificate' if you have to know what an adjective clause is rather than to be able to recognize prejudice in the reporting of an international incident.

Unfortunately, because these Certificates of Secondary Education will become, as time goes on, the passport not

only to employment, but also to Technical Colleges, more
and more youngsters will stay on at school beyond the age
of 15. This will then be hailed as a great educational
success brought about by the examination. But unless
the studies required for the examination have been enjoyed
by the pupils, and unless, as a result, they have acquired
a taste for learning and a strong desire to continue to
study and to understand some of the developments around
them, the success will be nothing but a hollow sham,
misleading the majority of the general public and also the
administrators.

As for the preparation for these certificates, it will not, in
general, help the teacher or the pupil to discover the pupil's
spectrum of abilities or his creative powers; for, as the work
of Professor J. P. Guilford has shown, academic attainment
tests favour memory and conformism.

What is needed by the secondary school pupil is 'educational
guidance' designed to reveal his full range of powers and to
help him develop those which will be of most advantage to
him. In Professor Guilford's words: 'If each child is to be
given the opportunity to make the best of his outstanding
assets, those outstanding assets will have to be recognized.'
Many of those assets are not the sort of gifts which the typical
written academic style examination is likely to reveal among
boys and girls most of whom, for environmental or other
reasons, have already been judged 'non-academic'.

As for setting up the sort of individual guidance and help
to our secondary school pupils which the Americans had
established thirty years ago, which would have enabled us to
shape our secondary schooling to the 'age, ability and aptitudes' of the pupils, we have done nothing. The matter is
discussed more fully in another chapter. Here we can only
say that our British respect for authority and for great names
at home has blinded us to the achievements of other nations
and put us upon a road in secondary education which is leading
us right away from the destination intended in the 1944
Education Act.

Return to the question of reserve of potential

The upshot of all such considerations is, in fact, that there is so much wrong with our present secondary education that nothing could be more absurd than to attempt to draw any firm conclusions regarding the human potential of our country from a survey of existing achievements of any sample cross section of our population of young people. We just have no conception of what the bulk of our flesh and blood stock is capable of, provided that it receives:

   (*a*) a primary education which is kindly, sympathetic and directed to drawing forth the inherent gifts and possibilities of the child, and then

   (*b*) a secondary education which is truly adapted to the needs of every individual child.

This is our final answer to the 'barrel-scrapers'.

CHAPTER THREE

What's Wrong: The Methods of Shaping Educational Policy in England and Wales

WE may well ask how it is that things have gone so badly wrong in our secondary education. If our answer deals unkindly with some who shaped policy, we can answer, with Thucydides: 'Why should we dwell reproachfully upon the past except in the interests of the present?' And, we would add, 'the interests of the future'.

It is the custom in this country, when future policy is to be thought out, to appoint a Commission of carefully chosen persons who are to invite and collect information and opinions, to examine witnesses and to produce a considered report. On the face of it, the system is a good one and many worthy reports have resulted. But things may go wrong: the constitution of the Commission or Committee may be such as not to cover all important fields of knowledge involved, and so on. Or there just may not be enough available facts.

Such a 'going-wrong' occurred, in my view, in connection with the Report on *Curriculum and Examinations in Secondary Schools* which was published in 1943.

The Committee was presided over by Sir Cyril Norwood, a highly distinguished classical scholar who had been successively Headmaster of Bristol Grammar School, Marlborough College and Harrow School, and subsequently President of St. John's College, Oxford. The tragedy of this Report is that it consolidated in the minds of important educationists—especially administrators—all over the country the belief that the tripartite system of schools (Grammar Schools, Secondary Technical Schools, Secondary Modern Schools) was the best possible system. This matter is treated more fully in Chapter 7, and a possible partial explanation, not unconnected with classical studies, is seen to emerge. The fact, however, that this Committee of highly respected and influential men and women should have given their assent to a discovery regarding the division of young adolescents into three distinct groups (see p. 83), which had hitherto eluded psychologists the world over, is an amazing one. But it is noteworthy that no educational psychologist was a member of the Committee and, in the List of Bodies that submitted Memoranda or otherwise assisted the Committee, no Body of psychologists is mentioned, though those listed range from the Institute of Actuaries to the Institution of Naval Architects. In contrast, the Consultative Committee presided over by Sir Patrick Spens,which reported in 1938, had made abundant use of at least four of the leading educational psychologists of the time, and that Report is still regarded as a document of great value.

We must not suppose, however, that this blunder was to be the last error of great significance to be made by an important advisory committee. The Central Advisory Council for Education, presided over by Sir Geoffrey Crowther, an eminent economist, produced in 1959 an extensive report, most of which has been rightly praised. Nevertheless, this group of distinguished men and women, assisted, of course, by administrative officers of the Ministry of Education, in the section of their report dealing with the Sixth Form, fell into the same trap as the Norwood Committee. Accepting uncritically a situation which has grown up to meet administrative convenience, and without any scientific evidence to support their conclusion, they, like Norwood, divided young people into certain clear-cut categories. And, purely as a result of their discussions, they discovered an aspect of human development which had hitherto, like some rare element, defied isolation. Just as a scientist discovering a new substance may himself give it a name, so the Central Advisory Council gave the name to the phenomenon of adolescence which they, in their deliberations, had perceived. They named it 'subject-mindedness'.

They defined it in the following way (Section 333):

> If 'subject-mindedness', a special devotion to a particular branch of study, is a vice of teachers . . . it is a virtue among pupils. It is the spring from which the disinterested pursuit of knowledge wells.[1]

Then, in Section 387 they elaborate upon this in the following words:

> The first step in the argument for specialisation is that able boys and girls are ready and eager by the time they are 16—the ablest by 15—to get down to the serious study of some one aspect of human knowledge which, with the one-sided enthusiasm of the young, they allow for a time to obscure all other fields of endeavour. 'Subject-mindedness', as we have already noted, is one of the marks of the Sixth Form. It is there whether we use it or not.[2]

It is to be noted that the last sentence quoted[2] here is an affirmation very much of the same kind as given in the Norwood Report with regard to the three types of adolescent (see Chapter 7, p. 84). It implies that the dichotomy of the Sixth Form in England and Wales into two groups, Arts and Science, is a natural one corresponding to the urges felt by the young men and women themselves. It is not, on the Crowther thesis, a result of the way in which the English Public School and Grammar School curriculum has developed, but a phenomenon which, presumably, is a human one, and not confined to English and Welsh boys and girls.

This important discovery in the field of the psychology of the 'gifted' adolescent must, we might suppose, have caused considerable consternation, not to say jealousy, among continental psychologists and pedagogues, whether in France, Germany or Scandinavia. For the nature of the studies of young men and women of comparable ability and age in these regions has been based upon diametrically opposite assumptions.

Fortunately, it was not left to foreign educationists to challenge the Central Advisory Council to produce evidence to support their contention. Instead, Oxford threw up another heretical Wycliffe, Mr. A. D. C. Peterson, Director of the Oxford University Institute of Education, who not only doubted the reality of 'subject-mindedness' but, with the help of his colleagues and the Gulbenkian Foundation, produced evidence, based on widespread investigation, that no such stage of natural adolescent development exists. Questionnaires were issued to nearly 3,000 boys and girls making a representative cross-section of Sixth Forms in England and Wales and to some 700 boys and girls in France and about the same number in Germany. Telescoping the detail we may say that the returns showed that if they were given a free subject choice roughly 70 per cent of boys and girls in all three countries would choose a mixture of Arts and Science subjects.[3]

The only possible conclusion is that the 'subject-mindedness' does not exist and was a figment of the imagination, invented by a member of the Council and seized upon by the remainder present on that occasion as a means, conscious or unconscious, of justifying developments which had already taken place and of ensuring their continuation without change. This had also been, in effect, the conscious or unconscious intention of the Norwood Committee with regard to the tripartite system of secondary schools.

The blunder of the Crowther Report would be less reprehensible if the situation which they were defending had been a good one. Consider the views on the Sixth Forms put forward by Mr. Percy Wilson, C.B.E., H.M. Senior Chief Inspector, in the Presidential Address to the Education Section of the British Association for the Advancement of Science in September 1962. His subject was 'The Unity of Knowledge: a new dynamic for the schools':

Our Sixth Forms are now specialised to a degree unknown elsewhere in the world and to an extent that would shock us if we could look at them, not with our present eyes that have grown gradually used to the pattern, but with our eyes of twenty to thirty years ago. . . . It is specialisation in density: in facts and dogmas, with neither breadth nor depth, nor height nor any other creature to recommend it. To ignorance of two-thirds of the curriculum it adds a factitious congestion of ill-digested over-information about the other third. It is anti-cultural as well as uneducational. It dis-prepares, rather than prepares, the boys and girls for the real business of university study, and equally for the real business of technology, commerce and the learned professions.[4]

There could hardly be a more sweeping condemnation of our present degree of specialization in the Sixth Form. And yet this is what Crowther would have fixed more firmly upon us but for the temerity of Mr. A. D. C. Peterson.

It should also be noted that Mr. Percy Wilson was Senior Chief Inspector at the time of the deliberations of the Central Advisory Council. The list of witnesses given in Appendix I is confined to persons outside Government Departments. So we do not know if he was consulted by the Council.

Is our present method of establishing educational policy a sound one?

The two serious blunders on the part of Advisory Committees which were asked to formulate vitally important educational policy lead one to ask whether this method of giving guidance to the nation is a sound one. If the general principle is sound, then one cannot help wondering whether there are not recurrent weaknesses in its application and whether some (scientific) refinement of method of carrying out the principle is not required.

As long ago as 1950, in a lecture on 'The Scientific Background to Educational Change',[5] Dr. Rex Knight, Professor of Psychology at the University of Aberdeen, expressed somewhat similar doubts about the way in which the Advisory Committee system operates and produces its results. He said:

Many important educational changes have had no scientific background. Unlike most developments in medicine, they have not resulted from the practical application of facts and principles revealed by research. Some have been due to changes in our circumstances, or our ruling political, social and educational ideals; others have reflected the views, not necessarily scientific, of forceful Advisory Committees and individuals.

After naming three such changes which were without scientific background he continued:

A fourth educational change that owes nothing to science has been the establishment of the three types of secondary school; the Grammar School, the Technical School and the Secondary Modern School. The only connection between psychologists and this innovation is that they have vigorously attacked the ground on which it was recommended by the Norwood Committee. Thus they have pointed out that there is no evidence for the suggestion that a definite stage of growth begins at about the age of eleven, or for the crucial statement that the three types of school correspond to three distinct types of mind clearly discernible among children of eleven.

Burt and Schonell are only two of the psychologists who have exposed the fallacies underlying this strange excursion into typology. Schonell refers to it as 'perhaps the most outstanding example' of the fact that in British education 'too often and too strongly does mere opinion hold the field instead of information gathered from observation and experiment'.

The tragedy is that millions of children have suffered and continue to suffer from factors of the Secondary Modern School because, except by adopting the Leicestershire Plan[6] (discussed in Chapter 7, p. 74) it is difficult to prevent a school building, once erected, from dictating the local system of secondary education.

Review of the situation

Reviewing the situation in which English education finds itself we are bound to be highly disturbed. Firstly, there is no long-term planning seeking to connect education with the social and economic development of the nation.

Secondly, when developments or changes are required guidance is sought from Advisory Committees of distinguished

3

persons who, it would seem, are provided with inadequate professional guidance and objective scientific information.

Thirdly, in the political circles which control the nation's expenditure there is no real acceptance of the twentieth-century truism that in the last resort it is the nation's schools which determine the nation's destiny. As a consequence all education is conducted with the utmost parsimony.

Research in education

Regarding research in education there has been no vision at all. Perhaps some members of the Central Advisory Council were feeling a lack of factual information when in Section 697 of the Crowther Report they wrote:

> In view of the very large sums of money that are spent on education every year, the expenditure on educational research can only be regarded as pitiable. If there is to be a consistent programme of educational development, almost the first step should be to review the provision for statistics and research.

Yet on April 19th, 1962, Mr. James Boyden, Member of Parliament for Bishop Auckland, after quoting Section 697 and saying, 'I am aware that the Minister is doing something about this', went on to point out that in the education bill for £800 million only £150,000 is spent on research, and added that 'even if the figures were doubled, what is being spent on educational research is what meteorologists call "trace". The Department for Scientific and Industrial Research makes a grant for research into whitewash almost as great as the right honourable gentleman does in educational research and it makes a slightly larger grant for research into glue.'

Although some slight increase may have taken place after April 19th, on December 2nd of that year Dr. B. V. Bowden,[7] Principal of Manchester College of Science and Technology, calling for a change in the 'curious and illogical' financing of education pointed out that Britain spends less on research into the improvement of education than the Department of Scientific and Industrial Research spends on improvements in the manufacture of nylon stockings.

Because of the influence of wealthy charitable foundations in the U.S.A. comparisons with expenditure on educational research there are not fair ones. But when one considers that $4 million have been spent most valuably in the last few years on the improvement in the teaching of just one subject—biology—one glimpses the possibilities that exist for improvements in teaching in all subjects that will make many existing methods look antediluvian within the next few years.

The example of Sweden

In the year 1940, Sweden, in the precarious position of a small neutral nation, decided that her existence in the years ahead was dependent not only upon her making the utmost of every individual citizen by enabling him or her to develop his potential gifts and qualities as far as could be made possible, but also on having a united community. It was admitted that the existing system of education, though highly democratic, was, by many, considered not to offer equality of opportunity and that alterations were necessary. So a School Committee, *a specialist body*, was set up to accumulate factual information and expert opinion. Adequate funds were provided for extensive investigation and research in various parts of the country, including notably a full-scale investigation into the interests, abilities, aptitudes, physical powers and so on, of adolescents in all the schools of the city of Gothenburg, which has a population of 400,000. This work was conducted by an expert team working with the teachers of the schools and the whole scheme was directed by Professor Elmgren, the distinguished educational psychologist of the University of Gothenburg.

It is important to point out that the collection of the necessary results and data took six years. Then the Swedish School Reform Commission, with Dr. Ingemar Düring, Professor of Greek in the University of Gothenburg, as Chairman, was appointed. Most of the members were not educationists, but the material, with recommendations from the School Committee, upon which they had to work was professionally sound. The Commission also made investigations into education in other countries and within four years its main recommendations were enshrined in the School Reform Act of 1950 which was passed unanimously by Parliament. But the last of its reports was not completed until midsummer of 1952 and then the Commission closed down. Its task had been to fix long-term lines for the development of education and no effort was spared not only to accumulate all relevant information and to reflect upon it, but, during the process, to encourage widespread debate and discussion upon the proposals so as to prepare public opinion for change. The printed reports alone run to over five thousand pages and the Swedes claim, probably correctly, that this is the most comprehensive and profound study that any nation has made of its educational system.

It would be inappropriate here to discuss the details of the Reform, but the central feature of sweeping and far-reaching changes in education and its methods was the introduction of the Comprehensive Middle School, keeping for nine years in the same school all pupils to the minimum leaving age of 16+ (*i.e.*, the end of the school year in which the pupil reached the age of 16) but providing for about half of them some pre-vocational studies in the last two years. The change was introduced gradually, at the initiative of what in England would be called Local Educational Authorities. It has met with such success that the localities have been hastening the change-over and by 1968 the whole of Sweden will have adopted the new system.[8]

Meanwhile a further School Commission, which is still in being, was appointed in 1957 to have oversight of experiments, to issue reports, and generally to guide the developments of the next few years, putting, when desirable, new recommendations to Parliament.

Of course in a country in which the total population is only 7½ millions change may be easier to bring about than in England and Wales with a population of 46 millions. On the other hand the provision of education is fraught with difficulties in many parts of Sweden, for the area of the country is 173,000 square miles compared with the 58,000 square miles of England and Wales.

But the lesson which we in England and Wales should learn from Swedish reform is the need to base change upon evidence gathered with extreme care and scientific accuracy rather than allow currents of mere opinion to decide our future.

CHAPTER FOUR

Civilization, Education and the Family

The nursery years

'IT was within the family', wrote Edward Glover,[1] 'that love scored its first real triumph by holding in suspense the hates and rivalries that would otherwise have broken the family asunder and so reduced its chances of surviving. It is within the family that, generation after generation, civilization is reborn.'

Social history shows us that Edward Glover's words are no lyrical over-statement; they are in fact a sober appraisal of what really goes on beneath the surface in providing the leaven for a society whose institutions are suffused with mercy and a measure of kindliness. And when crime and individual disorder begin to increase, or continue to increase, we need to turn our attention to the quality of the home life which these socially disturbed people experienced in their childhood and to consider whether the general home life of the present gives evidence of improvement.

Religion, of course, has long sanctified the family and the Christian religion perhaps most of all, until of late. Since the First World War, however, some forms of Protestantism may seem to have allied themselves very often with business, to have become caught up too much with ideas of productivity, material possessions and family restriction. So the leaving of the little child in the creche or in the nursery school while the mother goes out to work is condoned and they do not emphasize, as the Roman Catholics have never failed to do, even when war campaigns called the mothers to make munitions, that the purpose of marriage is matrimony and that the greatest achievement of womanhood lies in the bringing up of a God-fearing family.

As for the psychologists, they have never minced matters regarding the importance of the mother in the home and her concentrating on her task of caring for her little ones. One of Adler's most important statements is the following:

Every marked attitude of a man can be traced back to an origin in childhood. In the nursery are formed and prepared all of man's future attitudes. Fundamental changes are produced only by means of an exceedingly high degree of introspection or among neurotics by means of the physician's individual psychological analysis.[2]

Long before Adler, of course, other great minds throughout history had stressed the importance of the nursery years, Plato and Aristotle being outstanding examples.

Then we shall persuade nurses and mothers to tell those selected stories to the children. Thus will they shape the children's souls with stories far more than they can shape their bodies with their hands.[3]

Or, in the words of the great Czech educationist, Comenius: 'By what men learn at their mother's knee do men live and die.'

Of recent years University Institutes of Education, through all their constituent bodies, have helped to make known to all teachers the scientifically established fact, now so carefully based upon case studies as to be incontrovertible, regarding the irreplaceable part played by the mother, particularly in the earliest years of the child's life. Dr. D. R. MacCalman, Professor of Psychiatry in the University of Leeds, says:

When an attempt is made to compare the healthy with the un-healthy personality, we are struck by the presence of a sense of security . . . in the former and its absence in the latter. Various authorities have attempted to explain this difference in several ways, but all are agreed that this basic attitude, towards oneself and the world around, is derived mainly from the experience of the first years of life. . . . Basic security, this 'cornerstone of a healthy personality', is therefore directly dependent upon the quality of the relationship which the baby makes with his mother.

It should be close, warm, continuous and satisfying to both, for when the symbiotic relationship is first severed, the baby is dependent upon his mother to a degree and extent which we are only now beginning to understand. It is not only that his physical growth, and even his physical existence, is dependent upon mothering, but his capacity to pass through the difficult early stages of personality development is also bound up with this first and fundamental human relationship. Bowlby[4] has called the mother 'the psychic organism', for she is, to begin with, his ego and his super ego. Through her alone he is able to develop from a stage at which he is wholly a slave to his instincts and dominated by the pleasure principle, to the stage of adult adjustment when he can harmonise his inner needs to the demands of external reality. The success or failure of this long, slow subtle process of personality development is related more closely than we ever realised before to the critical phases through which the child must pass in the first year of life.

In a sense, the needs and the reactions of the baby are more simple and easily satisfied than those of the mother. He needs to be nursed, and fed, and welcomed; 'he lives through and loves with his mouth; and the mother lives through and loves with her breast'.[5]

Rousseau had also perceived the connection between the nursery and good citizenship. Writing at a time when upper-class women put their babies out to be nursed by women of lower class, he wrote:

But when mothers deign to nurse their own children, then will there be a reform in morals; natural feeling will revive in every heart; there will be no lack of citizens for the state; this first step by itself will restore mutual affection. The charms of the home are the best antidote to vice.[6]

Of course, it is not merely the first year of life that counts: all the other years in the nursery stage are of great importance; deprivation of love or of a sense of security is always bad for a schoolchild or even for an adolescent, but in the pre-school age it is particularly damaging, often irrevocably.

But, still worse, the trouble does not end in the life of the child whose needs have not been met.'Deprived and unhappy children grow up to make bad parents,' says MacCalman.[7]

So it would seem that 'the sins of the fathers are visited upon the children unto the third and fourth generation of them that hate me' as the Mosaic code has it.

If, therefore, the purpose of education is the generation of happiness, it would seem an inescapable conclusion that the first objective in education is to minister to the needs of the family and in particular to the physical and psychological needs of the mother.

That we have moved a long way in this direction since 1945, thanks to the establishment of the National Health Service and the introduction of family allowances, is true, but until it is almost universally accepted in this country that the shaping of a human personality is the greatest work that any woman can be asked to undertake, women will continue to be tempted to sacrifice the child's inner life for their own outer satisfactions. It is, in short, merely a matter of getting things into proper perspective and, despite the false glamour in the suggestions of the cheap press, getting the right values established in society.

In this matter education can, almost surreptitiously, play a very big part. We need to let adolescents know, while they are still at school and under 15 years of age, that the psychological care of a baby is second only in importance to its physical care. We need to stress the full parental responsibility in this matter and the self-sacrifice that it must involve for the parents. This information needs, of course, to be given to boys as well as to girls. Any normal healthy boy between 12 years and 15 years of age, though he may not wish to admit it, is interested in babies and in very small children and may enjoy caring for them or playing with them. Yet in this same age range, even in these very modern days, he is unlikely to be seriously interested in girls, so this is the stage when such information regarding the basis of family life—love for and care of babies and children—can be slipped across, almost as an *obiter dictum*, in any of quite a range of lessons, such as literature, history, divinity, civics. But a good opportunity arises in the course of biology lessons, when the devotion as parents of different types of animal towards their offspring can be contrasted with the far greater demands upon parents of animals higher in the evolutionary scale, with man having incomparably the greatest responsibility in this field.

It might well be helpful, too, if in schools where so-called 'sex instruction' is given the matter were broadened under the heading of 'family affairs', so shifting the emphasis from the self-regarding sentiments to those of an unselfish and even altruistic nature.

These paragraphs are not to be interpreted either as a plea for the unrestricted family or for the old adage, 'A woman's place is her home'. As Ecclesiastes has it, 'There is a time for everything under the sun', and whilst there is a time when a woman's best contribution to society may well be made solely in and through her home, life in the last third of the twentieth century is distinctly different from that of any other period in history and offers, incidentally, to the woman whose children are no longer small, opportunities of service such as have never existed before. Moreover, much of this service she can perform better than anyone else. This matter of the social contribution of the middle-aged woman is discussed in some detail in a later chapter.

The need for changing outlook as social conditions change

What we have to do is to adapt our educational and sociological outlook to the new and ever newer circumstances that the passage of time is ceaselessly producing before our bewildered eyes.

Among these changes is the phenomenon—new for this century—of early marriage, especially among women. However, one should raise no lamentations over this new development; indeed, one should rejoice and look forward to the new possibilities that it opens up. In terms of sheer physiology there is nothing to be deprecated in women bearing children while they are young, indeed, at as early an age as 18 years. It has been done successfully over a vast period of time over vast areas of the earth's surface. And today there is incontrovertible medical evidence not only that both boys and girls are maturing earlier than they used to do in this country, at any rate during the current century, but also that young people are taller and heavier than their fathers and mothers were at the same age. Moreover, not only is childbirth generally easier for the young woman who has borne her first child before the age of 23, but it may well be that in the early twenties she is better adapted psychologically for all the nervous strain which is inevitably entailed by several little children running around, all demanding different forms of attention simultaneously.

The foregoing paragraphs might be regarded as advocating that schoolgirls should become mothers, but that is not the intent behind them. It is merely to urge that we should not do anything to oppose this fall in the age of marriage, even if it lies within our power to do so. Rather we should make the necessary adjustment in our educational provision in secondary schools, in further education, in the age of admission to teacher-training colleges and in adult education. The whole question of the impact of early marriage upon the number of women teachers is discussed in a later chapter.

Provision for care of the family in France

It is, perhaps, important to recognize that these changes, so far-reaching in the United Kingdom, are not peculiar to our own country. In France the Institut National d'Etudes Demographiques announced in July 1962 that 29 per cent of French women marrying nowadays are under 20 years of age and similar trends are to be found in most 'western' countries.

But we should also be aware that behind the earlier marriage phenomenon in France there lies something far more significant in affecting the rise in birth rate than exists in England. Since the end of World War II France has steadily maintained, despite many changes of Government, 'une politique de naissance'. Under this, family allowances have been far more generous than in this country and not subject to income tax and they have been supported by special concessions in shops and in buses and trains by reductions to all who carry the special card indicating 'famille nombreuse'. Moreover, the allowances are carried to a much higher age in France in respect of children pursuing full-time education. Consequently the effect upon education, and especially upon apprenticeship, which is catered for by a three-year course of full-time education, has been remarkable. For the continuation of the allowance encourages the parents not to withdraw their children from full-time studies, including full-time apprenticeship courses, before they have fully benefited from them. Yet the steady persistence of a high birth-rate, not much lower than that of the years of birth rate bulge, has not been followed by unemployment. On the contrary, French demand for labour has not flagged; indeed it has continued to grow.

Perhaps the full significance and contrast of the French post-war financial support for the family is best given by the following letter which the writer received from a French friend engaged in educational administration. It is particularly important because it emphasizes the French national support for the principle that the mother of small children be encouraged to stay in the home. Hence the much higher allowance paid to a family in which there is only one earner:

(1) You are right in saying that in France the allowance we receive for children is not subject to income tax (in fact, to no tax whatever).

This allowance is composed of two items:

(a) 'allocations familiales': they vary according to the number of children, and the scale is progressive (I mean that what you get for your fourth child is more than four times what you would get for an only child).

For my two children I receive 63.27 N.F. monthly. That might be withdrawn if the children missed school without any valid excuse for more than four half-days in the month. The Court would decide.

(b) 'allocation de salaire unique': paid only when the wife does not earn any money, and devotes herself to the care of her children.

This means for me 77.80 N.F. a month. Roughly, then, I get a little above £10 a month, which I would not get if I had no children. As I said this is free from all taxes.

Speaking about Income Tax, the number of children has incidentally an effect on the amount we have to pay. A single man pays more than a married man and a married man without children much more than the *pater familias* with three or four children. This difference may be maintained until the children are 25.

(2) The allowances —*i.e.*, both 'allocations familiales' and 'salaire unique', are paid for children who are receiving full-time education until the age of 20.

It should also be remarked that, as a result of the long-term socio-economic planning that has governed French life since the war, with education included as part of the socio-economic process, schooling has been provided for the rapidly increasing number of pupils, in spite of the added difficulty created by the increasing proportion who insist on staying at school beyond the age of compulsory schooling. Indeed, the proportion of young people between 15 and 18 years receiving full-time education is higher in France than in England and Wales.

But still more important is the fact that a law was passed on January 7th, 1959, whereby from 1967 all youngsters will be receiving full-time education—often practical or technical—to the age of 16+ —*i.e.*, ten years of schooling from the age of 6 years.

It is very important to stress that the words 'education' and 'schooling' in this French secondary school context do not mean that everyone to the age of 16+ will be receiving the sort of instruction traditionally associated with school, classroom and 'education'. While those most suited for it will take *l'enseignement général long* as preparation for university or technological studies of the highest level, others will take *l'enseignement général court* which will end at 16+ or 17+ and prepares for Training Colleges for Primary Teachers and for entrance to municipal, industrial and commercial offices. A third group, from the age of 13+, will take courses which gradually introduce higher proportions of technical studies during three, four or five years of preparation for a named technical qualification. A fourth group, the least intellectual, will have three years, from 13 +, of studies which, whilst based on general education, will be largely practical, with a wide variety of activities grouped under four different headings: (*a*) agriculture for boys, (*b*) agriculture with housecraft for girls, (*c*) rural crafts, (*d*) urban work, all of these giving, in the course of the three years, some actual contact with agriculture or industry.

These facts have to be presented—and some other countries too can also provide evidence of the same kind—in order to establish the point that long-term adjustment of education to economic and social changes *can* be carried out in a democratic community with very satisfactory results.

And in France, at least as much as in England, the family unit is basic.

The French scheme of using family experience to help the children

In building up her post-war services to the family France has recognized that there are four particular fields in which the woman who has herself produced a family can make contributions which cannot be equalled by any other members of the community. These are school medicine, liaison between school and family, counselling services to children at school and development and organization of holiday activities for children.

(a) Doctoring in educational establishments, including apprentice centres for both sexes

Recognizing the natural interest of women in the young and realizing that the experience of bringing up children would fall to many women doctors, France has put almost the whole of her school medical service, except the inspection of older boys, into the hands of women doctors. It is difficult to make fair comparisons, but it would seem that not only is there no serious shortage of school doctors in France, as in many parts of England, but that everywhere there is more school medical inspection than holds even in the more favoured parts of England and Wales and that it is extremely thorough.

In this country a large number of women who have qualified as doctors have been lost to the profession because opportunities of part-time work, such as that of school doctors on inspections, have not been readily available or adjusted to meet the woman's home circumstances. Indeed in July 1962 an enquiry was set afoot by the General Practitioners Union, under the direction of Dr. Patricia Elliott, a widow, to ascertain how many women doctors are at present not using their knowledge of the healing arts.

(b) The 'assistantes sociales' of educational establishments

In France the school medical inspection is not the spasmodic, formal and rather detached thing that it is in most English day-schools: something that helps the records and looks out for unsuspected troubles but is clearly no integral part of the school life. On the contrary in France the work of the school doctors is followed up and supplemented by the 'assistante sociale'—*i.e.*, a trained nurse who has, after experience, received special training for work in schools and in liaison with families. It is she who is regularly available to assist the teachers and also to follow up the doctor's instructions regarding individual children. Her liaison with the teachers is of particular value not only in cases of children who seem below par or depressed, but also in cases where homework seems regularly to be neglected and so on. She liaises with the school guidance counsellor and also with the health authorities regarding financial help for children who particularly should be sent to a 'colonie de vacances' in the summer.

(c) The school guidance counsellors

Still further to assist the child and the family, France has a system of 'school and vocational guidance' which takes advantage of the experience of women who have no longer any young children to look after. Until a few years ago the system was restricted to *vocational* guidance, offering, as will be explained in a later chapter, something very much more thorough than the Youth Employment Service is able to offer in England, despite all the dedication of its magnificent corps of men and women officers. For this Service in England, in the words of one of its own officers, is 'undermanned, underpaid and undertrained'.

The thoroughness of the French system demands much more generous staffing than in England and a large proportion of these counsellors are married women with family experience.

The guidance services inside school have grown up in France as one of the delayed effects of the Langevin Plan of Educational Reform which was presented in 1945. By 1955 it had become generally accepted that the diversion of young people along different streams of secondary education needs to be preceded by several years of careful unobtrusive study of every individual. This principle is now being applied, especially during the two years 11 to 13, which are now known as the 'cycle d'observation', and during which information is collected upon which to base definitive advice to child and parent. Hence the need, inside the schools, of guidance services. To meet this demand the vocational guidance service has been expanded to become the *Service d'Orientation Scolaire et Professionelle*. The counsellors assist the schools but are not, as in the U.S.A., members of the teaching staff who have undergone a series of training courses during vacations. Instead, they are rather more psychologically and sociologically prepared and, as already implied, women make up a growing proportion of the service. The training takes two years full-time: there is competitive entry from candidates who already hold a first university degree, the *licence*.

(d) *Holiday 'camps' for French schoolchildren*

For physical health, bodily exercise and the development of open-air interests and pursuits, France offers to nearly 1½ million young people under 15 a holiday every year at one of hundreds of permanent camp sites in mountain, in countryside or by the sea. These 'camps' may be of wooden huts or the adapted premises of former large houses or even former hotels or a combination of both house and huts. Tented camps are reserved for youngsters over 15 years of age. The holiday is of a minimum length of three weeks; more usually it lasts four weeks. Even for those who pay the full fee the price is almost nominal: for those children who are judged by the school authorities, including the medical ones, to require such a holiday there is no fee at all if the parental income is below a certain figure. In this work, too, though men play a big part, women play a greater one, for the 'colonies' are all for children under 15, each catering for a limited age range, but many of them being organized for children under 10.

Aspects of the work which call especially for the help of experienced women are the catering, the domestic responsibilities and the daily care of the health of the children.

Moreover, especially for the younger children, there is the careful organization of the daily activities which include a remarkable range of cultural activities as well as physical activities of all kinds. Under the experienced mature leaders of the colonies is a team of 'moniteurs' and 'monitrices' who are students or schoolboys and schoolgirls over 17 years of age. All of these have attended at least one special training course of two weeks: these are arranged in the Christmas and Easter vacations. Each moniteur or monitrice takes charge of a group of about a dozen children.

It should be noted that besides bringing remarkable aid to over a million homes every summer, these colonies involve tens of thousands of young men and women in common enterprise in the care of children—surely an admirable preparation for parenthood at a later stage.[8] Certainly in post-war social planning in France the family occupies the central place.

It should be added that for adolescents—i.e., young people over 15 years of age, there are the 'camps d'adolescents' which cater for nearly half a million young men and women. These are generally temporary tented camps offering fairly Spartan conditions and demanding strenuous life from the participants, though not generally at the level expected at Outward Bound Schools in England.

It must be stressed that the praise given to the *colonies de*

4

vacances must not be taken to indicate any forgetfulness or disparagement of the remarkable work done in the United Kingdom by voluntary workers in the provision of open-air activities for youngsters.

The Boy Scouts Association, the Girl Guides Association, the Boys' Brigade, the Girls' Life Brigade and the Youth Hostels Association are only the outstanding examples in a vast group of organizations of every size having somewhat similar aims.

But even some of these would be helped by the widespread provision of permanent hutted sites which would enable younger, and therefore more, children to take part.

CHAPTER FIVE

Nursery Schools and Infant Schools

THE United Kingdom is the only major country in which the age of compulsory school attendance is five years. In France and the U.S.A. it is six years, in Scandinavia and the U.S.S.R. it is seven years. No doubt Englishmen can explain the situation in terms of our higher intellectual endowment calling earlier for satisfaction! Whether they can show that at the age of 21, or even at the age of 15, there is any intellectual gain from this procedure, is doubtful. No comparative data are available, but if British children were in advance it would have become apparent long ago.

Yet 5 is clearly a satisfactory age since, below the 6th- or 7th-year entry, there are private fee-paying kindergartens in Scandinavia and the U.S.A. and state-provided kindergartens, also fee-paying, in the U.S.S.R., and France has free state-provided *écoles maternelles*. No doubt these other countries would like to fix 5 years of age for school entry, but, save France, they have not our inestimable advantage—our mild winters. Indeed, if we objectively tot up our relative freedom from snow, ice and flood, our relative warmth when parts of the U.S.A. are at a temperature well below zero Fahrenheit, our football fields almost always 'playable', and so on, we have to concede that English schoolchildren have a fortunate start and we can understand Tennyson, in Victorian imperialist mood, thanking

> Him who isled us here and roughly set
> His Briton in blown seas and storming showers.

Also, we must marvel that, considering the climatic handicap of children in northern Sweden, Finland or Russia, they catch up with English children so quickly.

It does not follow, however, that the extra year or two of schooling, consisting today as it rightly should between the ages of 5 and 7 more of play and social training and physical self-discovery than of formal learning, is for the child wholly advantageous. By coming out of the family and neighbour groups he is exposed to new flora of infection and it is possible that the English child between 5 and 6 years has more infectious illness than, say, children in Denmark or Norway.

It is also possible that the earlier social grouping may result, later, in more conformism than is found in the child who grows up outside the school system to the age of 7 years, as many a Scandinavian child will continue to do. Books he will have at home; culture will surround him even in a hamlet; but he will be more a child of Nature than, for instance, a Russian child who enters kindergarten at the age of 5 and who rapidly becomes, in that gentle, persuasive, semi-clinical group climate, an almost indistinguishable member of the whole. A Norwegian Professor of Education known to the writer chose to live miles away from the town where he worked in order that his children should be so rurally placed that, at the age of 7, they were still required to attend school only three days per week. For him the ideal was that of Rousseau—the child growing up as a self-confident healthy little animal, with physical skills, keen observation and a mind of his own:

> The education of the earliest years should be merely negative . . . fathers and teachers who want to make the child not a child but a man of learning, think it none too soon to scold, correct, reprove, threaten, bribe, teach and reason. . . . Do better than they. . . . Exercise his body, his limbs, his senses, his strength, but keep his mind idle as long as you can. . . . Leave childhood to ripen in your children.[1]

In a similar vein, in the brochure issued by the Swedish Ministry for Foreign Affairs to describe the working of the New Primary School Statute, we discover the following interesting passage:

> The period of compulsory school attendance starts from the beginning of the autumn term in the calendar year when the child

reaches the age of seven. After medical examination and other tests the child, if found to be ready for school, may, subject to the permission of the school board, be admitted to a primary school or experimental school one year earlier. In Sec. 15(1) of the new statute there is a new provision to the effect that a private school may not accept children below the lower age limit for compulsory school attendance without the permission of the municipal school board. For this purpose a test of readiness for school attendance must be carried out in the same manner as for admission to primary schools or experimental schools. *The reason for this is that the development of the child may be harmed if it goes to school before it is ready to do so.* (The present writer's italics.)[2]

There is another aspect of Scandinavian hesitation about early schooling that is worth consideration—consideration which may be forced upon this country as a result of shortage of single women teachers of infants, aged 5 to 7, namely the half-day system. In Scandinavia the school day is not, for the early years, a 'full' school day from 9 till 3 or 3.30, but just the morning. This enables married women teachers who have children of school age to teach in the classes of the very little ones and to have nearly half a day looking after their home and family. It is also adequately long for most small children, for they find the excitement of mingling with a large group tiring, and to be quiet at home, resting or playing with their own toys, in the afternoons is beneficial for them. Indeed, in England mothers frequently find that little children, especially in the first year of infant school, return home not only exhausted but fractious as a result of their nervous fatigue and prolonged restraint during group activities. The suggestion, by no means new, that such half-day schooling for infants should be introduced experimentally was made in the House of Commons on July 13th, 1961:

Mr. Peyton asked the Minister of Education if, in view of the fact that in most European countries education is not compulsory until a child reaches the age of six years, he will consider making attendance optional until a child is six years old.

Sir David Eccles: No Sir, I do not think this proposal would be in the interests of the children or welcomed by their parents.

Mr. Peyton: Is my Right Hon. Friend aware that there are some parents who are genuinely concerned about their children's individual needs and that this might be worth looking at again, instead of brushing it off quite as lightly as he appears to have done?

Sir David Eccles: I can assure my Honourable Friend that the age at which children go to school is not a light matter at all but is one about which we often think with great care.

Mr. Ronald Bell: Will the Minister consider whether it is not desirable that parents who feel strongly about this matter should have discretion to keep a child under 6 but over 5 at home in the afternoons so that the start to school is not quite so sharp and absolute as it is at present? Will my Right Honourable Friend bear in mind that this is the practice at a large number of private schools to which children aged five are sent?

Sir David Eccles: My Honourable Friend is quite right in saying that the organisation of the school day is something that is always worth looking at, and I will bear the point in mind.[3]

Whatever lies ahead, enough has been said to indicate that what most English people have come to accept without question regarding the starting age for compulsory schooling should not be regarded as sacrosanct. Indeed, it may well be that a system of half-day schooling between the ages of 5 and 6, or even between the ages of 5 and 7, is in the best interests of the children. It would help the community in providing an adequate number of teachers and so would permit smaller classes. And it might help the homes of Britain by discouraging the mothers of small children from undertaking whole-day work. Probably a series of pilot projects by small County Boroughs in which the Local Education Authority and local industry could easily get together would be most helpful at this stage and would reveal practical lines of advance.

The demand for nursery schools stems, of course, mainly from the various campaigns to get the majority of women into 'productive' work. The first national drive of this kind arose during the 1914–18 War and can therefore be regarded as pathological in origin. During the subsequent period of the World Slump, with its terrible unemployment every-where, Hitler first eased the situation in Germany by giving financial inducements to women to leave employment and marry.

The Second World War, and its aftermath of rebuilding, brought about the second and third waves of exhortation to women to leave their homes and to enter factory and office. This pressure, of course, was highest in the U.S.S.R. where, even from 1917, the attempt to build up a nation met with a desperate shortage of men, who had perished in millions as the Tsar's 'steamroller' of flesh and blood had been hurled in vain, again and again, against German machine-guns. As for the shortage of men in the U.S.S.R. after the Second World War, only recently have figures been emerging to give us a better picture of the prodigious loss of male life in the appalling grapple with Hitler's armies. It was *essential* for the U.S.S.R. to take women's muscular power, to put the babies into creches and kindergartens, at whatever cost to their development; for without young mothers taking the place of some of the lost young men there could be no survival of the nation. But, as usual in the propaganda of Communism, the dictates of necessity are dressed up in the guise of high principle, especially after it was discovered how successful creches and kindergartens can be in conditioning the individual to live the collective life and to enjoy it. So in the U.S.S.R., or at least in the great cities of the Russian Republic, every pressure, social and economic, is put upon mothers to deposit their infants in creches or kindergartens, for the day, or even for the five-day working week, and to play their part in production of material things. No one, however, who has spent some hours in these stuffy creches and kindergartens, abundantly staffed with women doctors, women nurses, women 'child-occupiers', and seen the pale, listless, docile little inhabitants of these hospital-like institutions, can believe that this is a good way of rearing children. Nor do the mothers have any illusions about this: many women who can devise ways to evade having to take their children to the creche do so, if their economic situation permits, and the same is true for the earlier years of kindergarten.

There is another important point regarding Russian use of female labour which is not generally known outside the U.S.S.R., namely that no one in Russia *likes* to see women doing heavy manual work, whether forking manure in the parks or filling buckets with cement for men to lift. So if the visitor tries to photograph such activities every effort is made to dissuade him from releasing the shutter. 'This is only a temporary situation', he is told, 'we were so terribly short of men after the war, but now the situation is improving and soon women will no longer work like this.' Or one is told: 'As more modern machinery becomes available we shall not need so much manual labour and we shall have men enough.' And if one goes to the great Park of Economic Achievement, one sees there huge photographs of giant machines and of great automatic plants producing vast quantities of material with hardly a worker to be seen. The Russian can see, as we all can, that if those economic interests that control public opinion in the U.S.A. do not, in their self-protecting follies, overstep the narrow margins of safety, then humanity as a whole can look forward to a time when all women can be allowed to withdraw from economic life during the years while they are shaping the personalities of their little ones. As we have already shown, Plato had a clear enough conception of the power of mothers and nurses two and a half millenia ago. His pupil Aristotle, following his master's line of thought in this matter, went even further:

> The character of the stories, true or fictitious, which are to be told to children under the age of five, must receive the best attention of the officers called 'Inspectors of Children'.[4]

Much that goes on in the nurseries and kindergartens of the U.S.S.R. bears a remarkable, but fortuitous, resemblance to nursery life in Plato's 'Republic'. When the time comes, as it surely will, that the Rulers in the U.S.S.R. can trust the mothers to have the main share in the bringing up of their children (and this will be when the standard of living of workers in the U.S.S.R. approaches parity with that in Western Europe) I am sure we shall witness the sort of volte-face on creches that we have witnessed with regard to the reputation of Stalin. But even before that time the pressure upon women to hand over the rearing of their little ones to professionals may well have been reduced.

How much more, therefore, ought we in this country, aided by a kindly climate, a wonderful inheritance of industrial skill, and the cultural and almost untapped intellectual resources of a Commonwealth, be able to provide the mothers of the future with better homes, larger gardens, much larger family allowances, still better clinical facilities, greater opportunities of home help and whatever else is needed; more parks, with 'park aunts' as in Norway, more paddling pools and all that will minister to the wholesome upbringing of our future citizens.

We should also note that before long the need to use women for some of men's work will have passed away, as it would have done already if we were not still devoting so much of our national productive power to war preparations. If we as a nation are wise enough to reduce our expenditure on so-called 'defence' we can vastly improve the happiness of our people. Speaking at a Conference on the Education of Girls at Reading University in April 1962, Mr. M. L. Jacks, the distinguished educationist, said, following a reference to the present birthrate:

There is certainly going to be no shortage of manpower. I would suggest that there is rather going to be a shortage of woman power, that is of women able to do what women can do and able to do it well. In these circumstances would it not be wise to leave more of the men's jobs to men? Moreover, automation and other tendencies are going to make more leisure generally available. Who is to enjoy it? The men or the women? I would support the women, partly because idle men are more likely to fight than those fully employed (and this might therefore be a contribution towards the peace of the world) and partly because women need the time, and could use it well, for the making of good homes.[5]

Social planning and education, as we must continually reiterate, even if it be *ad nauseam*, must in the future go together to an extent beyond anything that we have known in the past. The New Towns, such as Hemel Hempstead, Harlow, Crawley, Bracknell, have given us an inkling of what can be done, but they have also shown us new opportunities which, before the New Towns themselves existed, it had been impossible to envisage clearly. This remark applies particularly to education for community leadership, and to training given, both to adults and to adolescents, in this field. It also applies to the provision for the constructive use of leisure for all ages, for the integration of youth activities with the work and life of Community Associations, so that youth can assume its share of responsibility for community welfare as soon as it is ready to do so.

With the planning of new towns, the redevelopment and re-planning of old ones, the well-thought-out provision for the needs of young married couples and their offspring, we should anticipate a falling-off in the pressure for the provision of nursery schools, except in those centres of dense population where slum clearance will not have been completed, or where the price of land is so high that the Local Authority has failed to purchase enough for parks and small communal green playgrounds for the children of tenements.

In the great cities, too, a new socio-educational problem is arising and is being tackled with varying success, and that is the problem of coloured immigration. This problem is simpler if tackled at the root—*i.e.*, if coloured children attend the same school as white children from the start no colour distinctions arise. Children are not interested in their companions' skins, but rate them merely as good or bad 'friends'. Even at a later stage these problems usually begin from above —but the problem has been solved in New Zealand and in the Caribbean. So it can be in Britain. Our excuse for raising the matter here is that it must be tackled at an early stage. Then the sole problems arising are matters of earlier maturation of coloured races which is quite another question. If the need for educational action is grasped by those who lead public opinion, then we are presented with a wonderful opportunity of showing the world that our English educational and democratic theories do really work. But if we miss our chance to do something better than has ever been done before in inter-racial education for both children and, most of all, adults, then much of our high-flown expression of faith will look like empty boasting. But this is a topic which lies outside the scope of this book and must be left to others.

We need, however, in this chapter dealing with the first stages of education, to look, finally, at finances.

Cost of nursery schools

The following figures give the comparative costs of nursery schools, per pupil, compared with the costs of other types of schooling:

 (1) London County Council. Figures given in August, 1962.

Type of School	Actual cost per place 1961	Estimated cost per place 1962/63
Nursery	£129	£138
Primary (infant and junior combined)	£56	£67
Secondary	£97	£120

The fairly steep rises are due mainly to the higher salary scales for teachers introduced in January 1962. The L.C.C. does not make any breakdown between different types of secondary school.

 (2) Slough Division of the County of Buckinghamshire. Costs per place, ignoring cost of amortization or school holidays, administration, advisory services, etc.

	Estimates for 1962/63
Nursery	£87
Primary (infant and junior combined)	£55
Non-selective secondary school	£81
Selective secondary school	£115

The higher cost of the selective secondary school is due to the high costs of sixth forms.

(3) Reading County Borough 1961/62.

	£	s.	d.
Nursery	107	11	2
Primary (5–11)	48	16	9
Secondary (all types)	87	16	7

These figures, and similar ones which could be obtained from other Authorities, indicate that, in general, it costs more to attend to the needs of a toddler in nursery school (and these needs are largely physical) than to educate an adolescent in secondary school. Since, other things being equal, the home is the best place in which a toddler can grow up, it would seem a wise step to do everything possible to make nursery schools unnecessary, thereby releasing teachers to ease the burdens due to the harmfully large classes in infant and junior schools.

Of course, in some slum areas nursery schools may be a necessity, but sociologists, social workers and educationists should co-operate to restore its proper position to the home.

Nursery schools, infant schools and research

It is clear that most of what has been written here about nursery schools represents a personal view. Opinions of a diametrically opposite kind are held even more firmly by other people and organizations have been founded to propagate these contrary points of view.

It is, of course, absurd that on matters of such fundamental importance to society there is no available corpus of factual knowledge which might reduce the influence of mere opinion in favour of something more firmly based. But because educational research has been given so little attention and has been so starved of funds in this country, we have no facts to which to refer.

At the same time it must be admitted that the accumulation of significant data in this particular field would not only be difficult but extremely expensive, involving a span perhaps of twenty years to answer all our questions. Here are some of the questions we need to ask: What are the results of attendance of small children (*a*) from the age of 3 years (*b*) from the age of 4 years, at nursery schools with regard to:

(1) the incidence of all kinds of illness, ranging from the common cold to diseases such as measles which are more harmful to younger children, and including all minor illness which may be associated with nervous disturbance?

(2) the development of self-confidence, both psychological and physical (as a result of play apparatus and group physical activities)?

(3) attitudes towards meals and towards different kinds of food?

(4) relationship with other children of similar age?

(5) relationship with older children and with adults, including their parents?

Clearly some of these things are going to prove extremely difficult to measure; large numbers not only of nursery school children but of suitable 'control' children will be necessary if any significance can be attached to the statistics which might emerge, and the isolation of the nursery school factor from all the many other factors involved is going to be extraordinarily difficult.

These represent short-term effects which might be measured from the age of 5 years up to the age of 7, while all the children are in the Infant School.

But we also need to know the long-term effects upon human personality of associating children with group experience and group control from a very early age. Just as the swaddling of babies is believed by Ruth Benedict and some other anthropologists to be conducive to the development subsequently of a compliant attitude to the group, with a greater degree of intraversion to compensate for reduction in extrovert qualities, so there *may* be effects of nursery schools which reduce both contrariance and initiative. At present we simply do not know.

Some commentators on the Russian educational system are of the opinion that early group experience promotes in the adolescent and in the adult a feeling of group solidarity which increases both tolerance and altruism. A large-scale international investigation, sponsored jointly by the U.S.S.R. and the U.S.A., might be a fascinating way of throwing light upon the question!

Meanwhile the Russians have, presumably, the conditions for some investigations of this kind within their own borders, for we may suppose that not all rural regions are yet well supplied with creches and kindergartens. Indeed, it is impossible to be absolutely certain how far those shown to visitors in the great cities are really typical: after all we in England are pretty selective in the schools we show to guests from abroad. At all events, the children that one meets in Russian primary and secondary schools appear, in superficial contact and under classroom observation, to be very much like children in other advanced countries, except perhaps that they seem keener on their studies and at least as friendly to strangers as one will find anywhere!

Yet such impressions are very subjective and are certainly not admissible as scientific data. Even if they are accurate, who could sort out, from all the many intertwined factors, the ones that are really responsible for this extra keenness on study and for the welcoming attitude of these Russian children? Only scientific research can throw light on such questions.

CHAPTER SIX

The Junior School

The size of classes

IT is an odd thing that for many years successive Ministers of Education have been at pains to emphasize success in reducing the size of classes in secondary schools and that Ministry policy has always been prepared to tolerate a considerably higher maximum class size for primary schools and to permit it to be exceeded. Current policy (*i.e.*, theoretically desirable) is thirty in secondary schools and forty in primary.

Two justifications may be advanced for this view. The first is that there is, during most of the school year, so much minor illness among children between 7 and 12 years of age that, even if forty names appear on the register, there will seldom be forty children present.

However, whatever the reasons or excuses, in 1961 the number of 'maintained' primary classes in England and Wales containing more than forty children was no less than 18,113 out of 127,949 classes.[1] This means, in terms of children instead of in terms of classes, more than one child in seven in publicly-provided schools was being 'educated' in a group containing more than forty children.

The second justification is that the relative size of secondary and primary classes which is acceptable is traditional or historically accidental. Earlier in this century secondary education meant 'Public School' or 'Grammar School' type of education, which at that time demanded smaller classes than primary schools for two reasons. Firstly, the studies were relatively advanced and demanded opportunities for individual participation by the pupils, as in the construing of Latin or in referring, in spoken French, to the pens of their aunts.

Secondly, these pupils were to some extent, and today largely are, the gifted minority on whose leadership the country will ultimately depend, so the nation could not and cannot afford to stultify the schooldays of such pupils by classes too large for effective teaching. These arguments, whether we accept them or not, were in all probability those that originally shaped policy of the then 'Board of Education' towards Grammar Schools, and the same ruling with regard to class numbers has, unconsciously so to speak, been applied to other forms of secondary education. Indeed, during the height of the post-1944 crusade for 'parity of esteem' among all secondary schools, it would have been highly inopportune for anyone to suggest that the criteria for class numbers in Secondary Modern Schools should be different from those in Grammar Schools. But there is no reason why they should be.

So we now witness the interesting situation in which children over 12 years of age tend, by and large, to be in smaller classes than children between 5 and 12 years of age or slightly less than 12. In January 1961 there were 2,017,888 primary school-children in classes over thirty-five, but only 588,709 Secondary Modern youngsters in classes of this size.[2] Yet it is the young children who, most of all, need small classes for, though all youngsters under 15 or 16 need the pastoral care of the professionally trained teacher, it is the little child who needs this most. It we are brutally frank with ourselves we have to admit that the adolescent at school, especially the adolescent who is voluntarily staying on beyond the age of 15, has really only two important criteria by which he or she evaluates the teacher. The first is: 'Does he know his stuff?' and the second is 'Can he teach?' All other criteria, even regarding personal kindliness, are subordinate. Consequently the average adolescent does not welcome pastoral care unless it is extremely unobtrusive; even then it is unlikely to be acceptable unless the teacher has already scored high marks in the two main tests by which he is judged.

The child in the primary school, however, especially before the age of 10 or 11, is scarcely in a position to estimate the knowledge of the teacher, so much greater is it than his own. Still less can he distinguish the teacher's powers of exposition from the difficulty of the subject matter. To him the way in which he is handled, the kindliness, patience and restraint of the teacher, these are what really matter, together with the interest which the teacher shows in the child's affairs and his prattle. The teacher with a large class cannot fulfil these functions satisfactorily unless she is superbly gifted for the work; naturally only a small proportion of teachers can come under this heading.

The first desideratum, therefore, for improvement in primary education would be substantial reduction in the size of classes, with the Norwegian maximum of thirty rigorously enforced. This, in 1961, would have applied to 3,019,341 children in primary schools out of a total of 4,132,542 primary school children. Clearly such a transformation is utterly impossible at present; we are already desperately short of primary school teachers and to reduce the size of these classes to thirty children would require immediately an additional 25,000 primary school teachers. And our present production rate barely keeps pace with needs on the present staffing ratio.

Individual development

One of the most important educational principles in a democracy of the British or Scandinavian type must be the free and unfettered opportunity for every child to develop his own maximum potential in his own way. This of course, is a very difficult thing to achieve and it would be idle to pretend that we have yet achieved this. We have been moving steadily towards this ideal for generations, but in this respect we still lag behind Sweden and Norway. Perhaps the British educational ideal of the twentieth century has never been better stated than by the late Sir Percy Nunn in his swansong edition of the classic *Education, its Data and First Principles*:

> We must hold that a scheme of education is ultimately to be valued by its success in fostering the highest degree of individual excellence of which those submitted to it are capable.... We shall

5

stand throughout on the position that nothing good enters into the human world except in and through the free activities of individual men and women, and that educational practice must be shaped to accord with that truth.[3]

As for the Norwegian outlook on education, this was displayed in all its heroic magnificence in the defiant declaration, read by every teacher to his class, when the Germans set out in 1942 to nazify Norwegian education, a declaration which was paid for—as all who read it knew full well it would be—by physical suffering. In this case it was the suffering of the hundreds of schoolmasters who were hounded into the hell ship to Kirkenes or to concentration camps.

On 9th February the Norwegian 'Teachers' Front' was established. I handed in my resignation because I was of the opinion that membership of the 'Front' would lay upon me duties which my conscience would not allow me to fulfil. I am still of that opinion and have recently sent the following declaration to the School Board.

I reaffirm my protest against membership of the Norwegian 'Teachers' Front'. At the same time, true to my conscience and to my vocation as a teacher, and in accordance with the wishes of my pupils and their parents, I must declare that I desire to continue my work. I request that this be made known to the higher authorities.

I made this declaration because to be a member of the Norwegian 'Teachers' Front' and to teach are two fundamentally different things. For the same reason *I am unable to recognise the Ministry's view that anyone who teaches is thereby a member of the 'Teachers' Front'*. 'Each child's soul that we unfold is a new province for the country', says one of our dearest national sons. We teachers, together with the home and the Church, have the responsibility of seeing that this unfolding takes place in Christian love and understanding, and in harmony with our national and cultural traditions.

We have been entrusted with the task of giving you children that knowledge and training in thorough work which is necessary if you are to receive full and many-sided development as human beings, so that each one of you can take his or her place in the community for the benefit of himself and others. We have been given this calling by the Norwegian people, and the Norwegian people can call us to account for it. We also know that the sum total of the knowledge and labour capacity which a country disposes of are the greatest and most durable of all its sources of wealth. It is our duty to protect those values. We would be untrue to our vocation if we did not devote all our energies to the service of this task, especially in this period of affliction through which we are now living. *Every restriction on the activity of the school undermines the foundation on which our people's future must be built.*

The teacher's vocation, however, is not only to give the children knowledge. He must also teach the children to believe in and desire that which is true and just. He is therefore unable to teach anything which is in conflict with his conscience without betraying his calling. Anyone who does so is committing a wrong both against the pupils whom he should lead and against himself. That, I promise you, I will never do. *I will never ask you to do anything which I consider to be wrong, nor will I teach you anything which in my opinion is not in accordance with the truth.* As hitherto, I will let my conscience be my guide, and I believe that I shall then be in agreement with the great majority of the people who have entrusted me with my educational duties.[4]

This outlook is amplified by a statement made by Nils Hjelmtveit, Minister for Church and Education in Norway from 1935–45:

It is an approved principle of the Norwegian schools that, in addition to giving the greatest possible scope for the development of the special abilities and gifts of the pupils, it is the aim of education to develop, as far as possible, the personality of the individual. The teachers are not allowed to try to mould the children in their own image or to make them think and feel alike, or to believe in the same ideas.

This principle of freedom of thought, belief and action under self-controlled responsibility is the basis upon which all the Norwegian schools are founded.

Sometimes—speaking to bodies of teachers—I have tried to illustrate this point by telling the old story about Alexander the Great's visit to Diogenes. At the end of the conversation Alexander asked the old philosopher if he wanted to ask a favour of him, now the master of the world. Diogenes answered: 'I have only one wish: stand aside so that the light and warmth of the sun's rays may stream down upon me.' Every teacher should be able to imagine the pupil saying to him: 'Don't stand in the light! Let the great truths and experience which have been gleaned through centuries of man's life and struggles, sufferings and hopes, and which have been given expression in the great works of great men, shine upon me without any colouring from you.' Here is the best guarantee against intellectual regimentation. Here is the surest way of obtaining a free, healthy-minded generation of men and women who will be able to gain an independent outlook on the problems of their time and yet be able to find their place in society, to realise that they do not live alone in the world but must adapt their lives and their actions so as to serve the good of the whole community—first in the small community of the family, then in the larger community of the nation, and finally in the great, all-embracing community which comprises all the peoples of the earth.[5]

Learning by discovery

This determination to let every child use for himself, and in his own way, the heritage of man and his personal experience of the phenomena of the Universe received its first uncompromising presentation in the *Emile* of Jean-Jacques Rousseau in the year 1762. From this book, banned and burned publicly, has sprung all modern studies of child psychology and the whole concept of child-centred education. Yet, unfortunately, one of its basic contentions, one that is essential to the fulfilment of the higher purposes, is in great danger of being forgotten, smothered, odd as it may seem, by American capitalism. American capitalism, as we all know, maintains its development by the creation of new wants, often by the exploitation of parental love for children and the sense of responsibility towards them and their advancement.

The scientific leadership demonstrated by the first Russian sputnik caused an anxious and very necessary investigation into the teaching of science in the American High Schools, and splendid scientific teaching in these schools and in

Elementary Schools is now going on as a result of the researches of the past few years. Unfortunately, however, this movement opened the way for the flooding of the homes of quite young children with gaudy, expensive, over-simplified 'science' books, telling the 8-year-old all about atoms, the ionosphere, nebulae and who-knows-what else in the realms of difficult intellectual concepts.

We could be content to allow our American cousins, despite all we owe to them, to suffer the salutary punishments that the capitalist control of their society brings upon them, were it not for the fact that we seem all too blindly to follow in their footsteps. For instance, many of the most common features of our economic life today were developed in the U.S.A. ten to fifteen years before they became widespread in this country; this applies to Commercial Television, hen batteries, 'broiler' fowls, super-markets, and even to the advertisement which in 1959 was placarded on hoardings throughout Britain—'Advertising introduces you to the best things in life, and is largely responsible for your high standard of living'. This self-same advertisement—which had undergone no change in wording in coming to England—had been plastered on hoardings over a great area of the United States some five or six years before.

So we hope that as our primary schools introduce science they will not succumb to the blandishments of gaudy textbooks purporting to explain concepts which are well beyond child-hood understanding. Indeed, the best teaching at the early stages seeks to respond directly to the child's questions and to fit his interests. So the proper approach is sensory, perceptual and investigational, leading only later to deductions and theory. The danger of the present drive for science in the primary school is that teachers whose scientific background is inadequate even for this early stage may turn to the type of textbook that offers the child easy information instead of challenging him to find out. If they do, not only will the ultimate effect upon the children be to poison the wells of their curiosity and to bring science teaching into contempt, but, far worse, it will have permanently weakened their capacity for independent thought, for building up confidence in their own powers of observation and judgement and for belief in man's capacity to live in a rational world.

An example of an approach to science in the primary school which would appear to be on unsound lines, is given in a publisher's advertisement . . .

> a new scheme for the teaching of science in primary schools which seeks to introduce the simple fundamental physical concepts so that children will see the world in terms of energy, atoms and radiation. The scheme aims at making a continuous build up, by repetition, of a scientific vocabulary.

For Rousseau—and probably for all educational thinkers of all time with regard to primary education—the key word is not 'books' but 'things'. Nearly 170 years after Rousseau wrote his *Emile*, his thoughts at last found official acceptance in England in the famous dictum of the report *The Primary School*, 1931:

> The curriculum should be thought of in terms of activity and experience rather than of knowledge to be acquired and facts to be stored.[6]

Every child in every primary school needs continual opportunity to see, to touch, to handle, to draw, to make. He does not need to be drilled with words; he will seek words fast enough when he has ideas to express; he will develop through speech all the basic requirements of literary power if he has exciting discoveries to tell of. As an attractive Norwegian proverb has it: 'A naked woman learns to sew.'

Of course, if the discovery and investigation of his environment is to be for some years one of the principal parts of a child's primary education, then clearly the child who grows up in the country has a manifest advantage. Also any class work of an investigational nature demands small classes; this argument, derived from the nature of learning, reinforces that based on the psychological needs of the little child.

But it would be quite wrong to assume that study of the natural environment is difficult in city and town schools. Fortunately our English preference for separate family dwellings means that only a small proportion of children are without some form of garden, however small, from which they can observe some of the stars after sunset, in which a wide range of living creatures from worms, insect larvae, flies of many kinds, butterflies, moths, beetles and snails to sparrows and blackbirds make their appearance. And there are relatively few city schools which are at any great distance from a park and there are few museums that do not lend to schools teaching collections of materials which may be handled, whether they be cocoa beans and cotton-seed pods or specimens of many common types of rock and mineral. All that is required, for the proper study of things, is a class that is not too large and a teacher who knows how to help children to observe. Of course every teacher in a primary school should have a wide range of interests and knowledge about *things* from the stars above, the atmosphere and creatures around us, the earth beneath and 'the water under the earth' as the Decalogue puts it. But this desideratum can be provided and some Training Colleges already produce teachers with the right outlook. This outlook is chiefly the willingness to go on learning and to learn *with* the children, never seeking to show an encyclopedic knowledge, but always admitting limitation of knowledge linked with a burning desire to know more.

In short then, if we are to adjust our primary schools, which by and large are already very good, to the changing needs of our times we need to see, among other things, more time devoted to observational and simple practical work in science, beginning with all the elements of the natural environment and then going on to such things as simple study and investigation, by the children themselves, of air, water, weather, the sky by night, magnets and the play elements of electricity. These things are already well developed in the primary schools of Bristol and in a number of other areas too. This approach not only is in keeping with the teachings of child psychology but it provides an excellent introduction to science studies in the secondary schools, in which, until comparatively recently, English schools, with their insistence on practical work by the pupils themselves, could claim to be as good as any in the world.

Reducing the time given to the formal study of English

From what subjects is the time for the primary school science to be found? There are several possible answers. The first is that if, as in some schools in Bristol, the scientific investigation is made the centre of interest with which all subjects integrate, then the problem, as such, does not arise.

As a general principle, my view is that the time must be taken from the English studies, since description, whether verbal or written or both, is an essential element of the early scientific studies; indeed, the two are indivisible. I am also of the opinion, supported by the results of a number of experiments by different teachers, that the English language studies not only will not suffer from less time devoted to their explicit and direct cultivation, but will benefit greatly from this indirect approach. One of the most oustanding early experiments in this field was carried out some thirty years ago in the Preparatory School of Cheltenham College by the late W. D. Johnston, who removed English, as a subject, from the curriculum and approached it indirectly through all other subjects including a wide development of environmental studies in the field of the descriptive sciences.

Since then, especially where project work has been introduced, many others have proved that a far better command of English is obtained when the pupil is anxious to write and illustrate his own 'book', which he identifies with himself, and of which he becomes very proud, than by any formal studies. Notable pioneer work in the secondary school has been done and is being continued today by Mr. A. W. Rowe, Headmaster of The Margaret Tabor Secondary School in Braintree, Essex.[7]

A foreign language

There is another side from which the attack on the formal study of English—or at least upon its unduly large portion of the average timetable—is already beginning to be mounted, namely from that of the 'modern linguists'.

Many educationists, over long periods of time, but more vigorously from John Locke (1632–1704) onwards, have maintained that a child should start to learn a second language as soon as he is fluent in his own. They have based this argument on their observations of children whose parents had moved from one country to another and so on. They have also argued on *a priori* reasoning, that it must be easier for a child to learn to recognize and to reject new sounds at an early stage of his development, when he is still highly imitative. And John Locke went further and advocated the 'direct' method, without the painful learning of a logical grammatical system as the opening stage of the process:

> As soon as he can speak *English*, 'tis time for him to learn some other language. This no body doubts of, when *French* is propos'd. And the Reason is, because People are accustomed to the right way of teaching that Language, which is by talking it unto Children in constant Conversation, and not by grammatical Rules. The *Latin* Tongue would be easily taught by the same Way, if his Tutor, being constantly with him, would talk nothing else to him, and make him answer still in the same Language. But because *French* is a living Language, and to be used more in speaking, that should be first learned, that the yet pliant Organs of Speech might be accustomed to a due Formation of those Sounds, and he get the Habit of pronouncing *French* well, which is the harder to be done the longer it is delay'd.[8]

In this passage we find all the main points which have been established by modern research. But until quite recently the entrenched forces of the pedagogues have managed to resist all attempts to teach a modern language in the right way at the right age. Even today, despite the publicity given to the highly successful experiment in teaching French carried out in primary schools in Leeds,[9] with financial support from the

Nuffield Foundation, opposition is only being slowly overcome, but many Authorities, thanks to Audio-Visual schemes reaching us from France and the U.S.A. are experimenting with control groups of children.

Probably 90 per cent of teachers, when it is suggested that 8 year olds should start to learn French, German or Russian, will throw up their hands in horror, exclaiming: 'What— before they can speak the Queen's English? You ought to come and hear how my little brats maltreat their mother tongue. That would cure you of talking nonsense about teaching them a second language!'

Unfortunately for the teachers who think like that, the writing is on the wall. The hunches—or insight—of the people like Locke have been vindicated by the School of Education of Harvard University on the one hand and the neurological work of Professor Wilder Penfield on the other. It is now established, beyond the possibility of doubt, that in the educational climate of the U.S.A., where compulsory schooling starts at 6 years, the ideal age of starting the study of a second modern language—if one starts it on a direct or semi-direct plan—is 9 years. Thanks to Professor Penfield[10] it is now known that those areas of the human brain which are associated with speech are, as had seemed natural to many people outside the teaching profession, most responsive when the child is young and begin to decrease in that capacity even during the years of primary education. It is therefore extremely desirable that the natural capacity for learning a living language by imitation while one is young should be fully exploited, especially in a world in which economic frontiers are being rapidly broken down.

In France too experiments have been tried at St. Cloud which prove conclusively that children can best acquire a foreign language between the ages of 8–11 years—and also later on between the ages of 18–21 years. A foreign language in this country is generally taught in the ages between.

In short, primary schools must soon, all of them, perhaps within a decade, teach one of the important modern languages other than the mother tongue to the bulk of their pupils. Other nations, or at least a number of them, are well ahead of us in this matter, and an international conference for pooling ideas on the subject was held at the U.N.E.S.C.O. Institute for Education in Hamburg in April 1962.[11]

In this country, thanks to the foresight and persistence of the late A. E. Titley, M.C., H.M. Staff Inspector of Modern Languages until December 1959, selected students from Training Colleges spend a period of their preparation in France attached to French Universities. Only Treasury restriction has prevented this scheme from developing as widely as it should have done: there is no shortage of suitable applicants, and the scheme should be extended to include Germany, the U.S.S.R. and even China.

Early in 1963 the Nuffield Foundation asked the University of Leeds to prepare a report on all existing schemes of teaching languages to children in primary and junior schools in Britain.[12] Of course, the introduction of a second language into the primary school involves alteration in the amount of time given to other things, but although the *universal* introduction of a second language will be a new departure, experiment of this kind is by no means new. Indeed, tribute must be paid to a large number of primary schools which, at different times in the past few decades, when they have had a competent member of staff and an adequate number of teachers, have taught a second language with a considerable amount of success. Today, fortunately, despite the teacher shortage, special developments are taking place in the teaching of French in some primary schools in Oxfordshire, Devonshire, London and Buckinghamshire and in East Sussex similar work is being attempted also in the teaching of German.

Of course, elsewhere than in England a bilingual situation in schools already exists, for example close at hand in Wales, and further afield in some African countries and in the Middle and Far East. We can, then, expect to see most children of the world grow up speaking a second language. What is at present achieved in the primary schools of Sweden, Norway, Denmark,

U.S.S.R., of some schools in the U.S.A. and some provinces of Canada and elsewhere, should not be impossible in the primary schools of other countries in the world. British children given the opportunity and incentive have presumably as much linguistic aptitude as say Dutch or German children. They must, however, be presented with an opportunity to learn another tongue in a manner appropriate to their age and interests.

But once again, so far as England is concerned, if such teaching is to be effective the numbers in primary classes must be greatly reduced. This, of course, brings us face to face with the problems of recruitment and training of teachers, a thorny subject which is tackled in another chapter.

CHAPTER SEVEN

The Secondary School

ONE of the tragedies of the teaching profession, as has already been suggested, is its inability to bring about changes within its own work. Largely, as has been implied, this is due to failure to give adequate attention to the sociological and political aspects of life. Often this has been due to the very conscientiousness, devotion and high principles of the teacher, but, for all that, the result has been lamentable inability to adjust, from *within* the profession, either the system of schooling or the curriculum. For instance, Professor Ingemar Düring, Chairman of the Swedish Reform Commission, wrote in 1951:

> It is quite easy to insert new items into the school syllabus, and thereby to adapt it to the needs of the times, without at the same time lopping away the inessentials. The latter operation, however, is unavoidable and always painful to many teachers, and this is the underlying reason for the opposition encountered by every proposed school reform from the champions of tradition.[1]

Changes have been brought about in England and Wales, as we have instanced, by the Reports of Committees and Commissions, on which the driving forces have usually come from political, economic or social group representation. But, so far as secondary education is concerned, the main changes have been the work of political groups within Local Education Authorities. The most controversial change, and the one which is having, for better or worse, far-reaching effects, is the introduction of the Comprehensive Secondary School. Unless there had been Labour majorities on the London County Council and on the other Local Education Authorities in whose areas the first comprehensive schools were constructed, we may be

fairly certain that this experiment would have been delayed
for some decades.

It is highly probable that the full extent of the loss in training of character and in the establishment of values, that results
from the mass education of the huge, unsectional school,
will not be fully realized for some years and by then it will be
too late to alter the buildings. But, fortunately, not all Comprehensive Schools are huge and not all are unsectioned buildings. Meanwhile what has become apparent, and this is the
greatest contribution of the Comprehensive School so far, is
that those lay persons who, for the past thirty years, have
shown their faith in man by their firm though honest doubt of
the expertise of the 'testers', were absolutely right. In 1955,
during his first term as Minister of Education, Sir David
Eccles as President of the Council of the National Foundation
for Educational Research made some very unpopular remarks
when addressing the annual meeting. Coming as an outsider
to education he expressed regret that the bulk of the efforts
of the Institute seemed to be directed towards ever-continuing
refinement of the process of selection of children. He would
prefer, he said, to see more effort devoted to research into
better methods of teaching all the children.

These wise remarks were, however, at least five years ahead
of opinion in most pedagogical centres, which were still bogged
down in the morass of tests with which the name of Moray
House, Edinburgh, is indivisibly associated.

Five years earlier Sir Herbert Read, in his *Education
for Peace*, had attacked the system in a pregnant paragraph:

> At present, everywhere in the civilized world, we educate to
> promote intelligence, to promote industry, to ensure progress.
> It is not merely a question of promoting what the psycho-analysts
> call 'reality adaptation'; it is to the reality of a competitive and
> divided society that, by existing processes of education, we seek
> to adapt our children. The aggressive instincts have a wonder-
> ful opportunity to discharge themselves, but it is against other
> children, in a ruthless struggle for places, for examination results,

for class promotion. We educate to classify—that is to say, to divide—and all our efforts are expended in the cultivation of distinctions.[2]

It is *not* possible, we now know, to discover, by tests given to children at the age of 11+, all the boys and girls who are capable of being trained for the learned professions with any such degree of accuracy as would justify the process. The Comprehensive Schools and the Bilateral Schools, and the old 'central' schools of London and elsewhere, have shown that the reserve of talent in the 'late-developers' is far greater than the intelligence-testers had made out and that it is not yet given to any man or woman to be able, by the skill of their measuring instruments, to predict the limits beyond which the achievements of the majority of boys and girls will not go— unless these limits are set remarkably high. Yet in the 1930's it was difficult indeed for those who opposed the 'testers' to produce enough evidence to hold them back. And even today there are still areas where the procedure of the 11+ examina- tion (sometimes well called in the past the 'catastrophic' examination) is almost the sole means of deciding the type of secondary schooling which the youngsters attending publicly- provided schools will undergo.

Secondary education in some other countries

Yet everyone knows that the 11+ examination is on the way out. Denmark, which used to have something of the kind, although accepting a far higher proportion of young- sters for grammar-type education than in England, got rid of the system some years ago. So did Sweden with its introduction of Comprehensive Middle Schools ten years ago. Norway, wisely, never had such a scheme, but at the age of 14 all youngsters and their parents received school advice regarding the nature of their continued education. But they were not compelled to take it. If, however, those whose parents insisted on their continuing grammar-type education, despite contrary advice, persistently failed to keep up reasonable progress, they had to withdraw. East Germany scrapped the system at once after the War; West Germany is rapidly getting rid of it by gradual extension of the Rahmenplan. Under this scheme children of 10+ years of age pass into 'promotion classes' of two years' duration between the primary and secondary schools. These classes are staffed with teachers from primary schools and from the different types of secondary school.

> At the end of these two years a recommendation is given as to the type of secondary school for which each child is suited. No examination is needed. The authors of the Rahmenplan claim that a verdict given after two years of observation will be more valid than the forms of selection used at present.[3]

Experiments on these lines are taking place in various parts of West Germany. For instance in Bergedorf, a part of Hamburg, children of 10-12 attend the *Mittelbau*—

> where, without examination, they will be taught in forms then separate for part of the day. The first two periods and the last of every morning are attended by all the pupils of the age group together, whereas the two middle periods are taken up with courses in which the pupils are divided into 'sets' according to their ability. During the two years, individual children are moved from one set to another until they have all found their level. It is then obvious what type of secondary school they should attend, and they have been sufficiently prepared for it. There are some 400 children in the *Mittelbau* at Bergedorf at present and parents and teachers are satisfied with the results.[4]

It is a very good thing that the 'catastrophic' examination at 10+ is on its way out in West Germany because the parental and child tension in that country, with regard to the examination and its results, are greater even than in the United Kingdom and child suicides at this tender age are not unknown among those who have failed.

At the same time the writer considers, for reasons which are implicit in the preceding chapter, that the Rahmenplan is not by any means the best way of handling the matter and that in any case it is applied at too early an age and must, in addition, give too much weight to the effect of the encouragement and support of the parents to little ones of this age.

France abolished the selection examination for entry to secondary schools as one of the measures of its Reform Law of January 7th, 1959. The examination was replaced by a two-year 'cycle of orientation' during which every child is carefully observed by a team of teachers. This team usually includes teachers from secondary as well as primary schools, and they are specially selected for the work. They are always helped by the school guidance counsellor if one is attached to the school or group of schools. At the end of the two-year period of intensive study of the children, advice can be given both to them and to their parents. Only if the parent considers the estimate of his child's ability to be too low does the child have to take a written examination.

Since any kind of selection of children for different forms of secondary education is a complicated and, in many ways, an invidious process, fraught with all sorts of possibilities of injustice and of error, when Horace Mann, in the nineteenth century, campaigned in Massachusetts for secondary education for all it was for a common secondary school. And this developed into the Comprehensive High School which became the pattern for the whole of the U.S.A. and Canada.

This scheme of secondary education was copied by the U.S.S.R. after the Revolution of 1917 and it has also been adopted as the system of the People's Republic of China with its 700 million people.

But the Comprehensive High School brings its own weaknesses when it reaches a great size and has a considerable age range. This often produces a situation in which those personal influences which are some of the most important elements of education are scarcely felt.

The Comprehensive Middle School of Sweden was developed partly because, as a small nation, Sweden could not afford to waste any of her natural talent. But also it was essential to have a closely unified nation, with no unnecessary cleavages

6

and that purpose was the main reason for the appointment of the 1940 School Committee.

In the words of the Chairman of the 1946 School Commission which examined the twenty-one detailed reports of the Committee:

> A reform that is to bridge the old gulfs in society must see to it that the educational system appears to all social classes as a homogeneous structure where there are broad highways for all the youth of Sweden and where every growing individual, irrespective of his social starting-point in life, can learn how best to utilise his personal qualifications for his future tasks. Such an aim is not reconcilable with a system of parallel schools, whether open or concealed.[5]

In such a climate of world opinion it is unlikely that the United Kingdom will be able to maintain for many decades more a system of secondary education which creates divisions into almost hermetically sealed compartments and everywhere in the country the 11+ examination will have to be abolished, and with it the bipartite or tripartite system of schools.

There are other ways of abolishing this system besides creating Comprehensive Schools, whether they are on the excellent but expensive sub-divided House plan which was permitted by the Ministry to Coventry during the time of the post-war Labour Government, or on the undivided building plan subsequently forced upon Authorities by Ministry ruling. One of these is the system of bilateral schools found in Oxfordshire, another is the slightly different 'bilateral-plus-specialism' system of the town of Reading and a third, which has met with great success, is that known as the 'Leicestershire Plan'.

The Leicestershire Plan

This system bears a superficial resemblance to the 3–3 system of Junior and Senior High Schools which is common in most states of the U.S.A., *i.e.*, three years in Junior High, three years in Senior High. In outline it works as follows: All pupils, without exception, transfer, under the Leicestershire Plan, to a junior secondary school at the age of 11+.

The school is known as the High School, the adjective 'junior' not being used. During three years of secondary education a gradual orientation process takes place, somewhat like that organized in France, and at the end of that time it has become pretty clear which of the pupils are going to enjoy, or to profit from, studies which, beyond the age of 15+, are going to be mainly academic. Parents, pupils and teachers confer together when the child is 14+ and he may then go on to the Grammar School if the parents so desire. But a condition of his doing so is an undertaking by the parents that he shall remain at the Grammar School for at least two years and that they will not withdraw him from school, as they have a legal right to do, when he reaches the age of 15. Of course this undertaking cannot be legally enforced, but it emphasizes to the parents, if emphasis is necessary, that there will be little gain to the child from leaving the Grammar School without having taken G.C.E. at 'O' level in a fairly wide range of subjects.

Those pupils who do not wish to go on to further academic studies after the age of 15+ continue in the High School to that age, but their course may now include both studies and practical activities having a definite prevocational nature, and they may continue these, and general education, for several years beyond the minimum age for leaving school.

One of the greatest advantages of the Leicestershire Plan is that it can, in many cases, be adopted at once and does not require the building of great new schools, as the comprehensive scheme does. An existing Grammar School can be 'fed' from five or six High Schools, since the classrooms formerly occupied by youngsters aged 12 and 13 are now available for pupils over 14 years of age. In fact, the age range of the Grammar School becomes almost identical with that of the traditional boarding Public School, especially because there is an escape clause which permits outstandingly brilliant children in the primary school to enter High School a year earlier than their peers, and then to move on to the Grammar School at 13+ instead of 14+.

High Schools are placed in the buildings originally designed

as Secondary Modern Schools, and thus they, and the Grammar
Schools, are kept at a size which permits the Head not only to
create a keen team spirit among his staff, but also to know
personally every pupil and something about that pupil's
background. These are some of the most important factors
which help to shape the imponderables in education and are
among the many advantages of small schools.

Diversity of glory

It is strange that although most of our Edwardian fathers
and grandfathers were familiar with St. Paul's pregnant words
regarding the difference in glory of the sun and the moon and
the stars 'for one star differeth from another star in glory', yet
so far as education was concerned they recognized, strictly
speaking, only one glory. It has been left to our administrators in
the second half of the twentieth century to permit the development, on a wide scale, of differing forms of education of adolescents. One of the chief reasons for the success of the
Comprehensive Schools in making education palatable to a very
large proportion of the pupils is the variety of provision that
is offered for different activities, the practical recognition that,
after puberty especially, interests and abilities of any group
of young people spread out and separate like the ribs of
a fan.

It is the different ways in which nations cater for these
divergencies of aptitudes, abilities and interests which form
the most fascinating comparative study of adolescent education.
Unfortunately, cool detachment becomes difficult when the
shortcomings of one's own nation—or its successive governments—are visited upon young school leavers finding themselves, in their thousands in some areas,[6] not only without
work of their choosing but without any job at all. This is the
result of failure of successive governments to plan ahead and
to integrate education and economic and social development;
such a situation, as we have already remarked, compares most
unfavourably with that in countries where, as in France and
Sweden, long-term planning has been accepted since the War.

We in England have not, even yet, recognized generally that every unemployed person is a blood-sucking parasite which society has itself fastened upon its own flesh. Educationally the key word to full employment of the young is 'Guidance', which is a bigger concept than that of 'Vocational Guidance' from which it has developed.

School and vocational guidance

Expressed very simply the function of 'Guidance' in the secondary school is, firstly, to help the pupil to discover his own powers and abilities and desires; secondly, to assist him to develop ambitions which are not only consonant with his gifts but also likely to find opportunities of satisfaction in the world of work; thirdly, to help him to make the right choice whenever in school work there is a choice of options; and, fourthly, to help him when he leaves school to enter the sort of work which will provide him with the greatest opportunity of personal growth and lifelong satisfaction.

Unfortunately, in this matter of guidance the United Kingdom lags badly behind many nations, as most people who have made a study of it are aware, or as any can see who turn to the *Year Book of Education for 1955* (Evans Bros.), which is devoted to this subject. Worst of all there is, especially among headmasters of day secondary schools, except Comprehensive Schools, a degree of complacency about guidance which is very disturbing. The worst situation is that in which the headmaster, despite all the other calls upon his time and abilities, considers himself competent, without other help, to advise his boys what type of work they should take up. Next is that in which a member of staff, without any special training or industrial experience, acts as 'careers master' on the fringes of his time. Both headmaster and careers master, if they are wise, will work constantly with the local Youth Employment Officer who should be brought into close contact with the school. But even this is not enough for, dedicated though the Youth Employment Officer may be, thorough as his or her knowledge of local industry and commerce may be, he or she usually works under three grave disadvantages. Firstly the general preparation given to a Youth Employment Officer for this work is scarcely impressive to a teacher who is a University graduate or even to a teacher prepared in a Training College. For in most cases the training of a Y.E.O. for his Vocational Guidance Diploma, if he has one, has had to be gained on the job. Often, of course, the Y.E.O. is himself a graduate, but usually not in any field related to his work, and no University qualification closely related to Vocational Guidance exists at present, though there is hope of such.

Compared with that of a School and Vocational Guidance Counsellor in France, who has had a two-year full-time course of training following a competitive entry of graduates, or with that of a Guidance Counsellor in the U.S.A., or in the little country of Finland for that matter, the training of an English Youth Employment Officer is inadequate. In practice it does not mean that *he* or *she* is inadequate; no more devoted and efficient group of men and women exist in any part of our social services than the Youth Employment Officers and they spare no effort to make themselves the most perfect instruments that they can for the vital work which they do for the nation. Remunerated on a Local Government scale which inadequately recognizes their responsibilities they nevertheless, because of the human appeal of their work, give up much of what would be their legitimate leisure to help to the utmost the boys and girls who need them.

The second disadvantage under which Youth Employment Officers labour is that they are too few, as has been mentioned in an earlier chapter. As a consequence they are compelled to give far less time to the young persons whom they interview than would be given in any other country known to the writer where a guidance system exists. And the third disadvantage is that, for the short interview which the Officer has with the adolescent, very few schools are able to brief him adequately. Generally speaking, the school knows well the character and personality of the adolescent and his abilities over the range of school studies, but outside of these studies the school (unless a small one) is usually unaware of gifts and potentialities, often latent, which would be very significant for his future as a wage earner or salaried worker.

In the U.S.A., where almost every High School has an adequate number of highly-trained guidance counsellors, one of whom has known each of a group of pupils since he entered the school, there has been continuous observation and recording of the child's development, interests and abilities over the whole gamut of possibilities, so that the entire spectrum of his gifts is known. Moreover—and this applies to every country where there is good guidance—the adolescent will have been gradually led to a pretty accurate appraisal of himself and, even more important, to a knowledge of the types of work that exist and are likely to go on existing for people having his set of aptitudes and qualities.

Of course, there are some schools in England and Wales— and they are, fortunately, a growing number—where a comparable situation exists, but they are altogether exceptional and there is at present no proper training available in this country for careers masters and mistresses, while the term 'guidance counsellor', which implies personal advice and assistance to pupils (including especially the 'difficult' ones) throughout their school life, simply does not exist in England. Meanwhile, as we have seen, the services of these trained practical psychologists are being used intensively in France in the school situation and particularly during the two-year period prior to the decision (which even then can be modified) regarding the type of secondary education most suited to the child.

It is apparent that in this respect great development must be hastened in our country. Firstly, the Youth Employment Service must be expanded, must be better remunerated and, by proper University courses of preparation (the one-year course at Lamerbey Park having been a most worthy forerunner), given proper professional preparation and status.

Secondly, in order that there may be much more fruitful co-operation between Youth Employment Officers and schools, we must set out to train for every school *not* a careers master or careers mistress but a guidance counsellor and, as in the U.S.A., guidance counsellors for primary schools as well as secondary schools.

We are likely to be able to profit from the best of our existing system if we recognize that, so far as placement in work is concerned, no careers master is likely to be able to compare with a Youth Employment Officer. This is not merely in regard to knowledge of the nature of industrial and commercial openings, but in regard to the actual conditions inside industries in the locality. If more Youth Employment Officers were appointed, schools would be able to benefit from much more thorough dissemination of information, by films and by visits, among their pupils regarding the rapid changes in the nature of the demands for manpower and womanpower which are taking place in this Computer Age.

Almost any report on employment today refers to the difficulty of using unskilled labour wherever large or small pockets of unemployment exist. Specialized skilled labour can often find openings abroad, as Rolls Royce workers in 1962 did at the Fokker aircraft works in Holland, and in other work in Switzerland; but for the unskilled and semi-skilled, as we have seen already, there will be ever-decreasing opportunities.

Moreover, all technical workers need to have a broad range of basic skills—what the French aptly call polyvalence —so that, if one specialism becomes redundant, the worker can fall back upon his broad range of basic skills and moving, as it were, to left or right of his original specialism, erect a new specialism for which there is demand. In England, with its two cultures, the very word polyvalence has no meaning for a large section of the so-called intelligentsia, for they have not the very elements of knowledge of chemistry which makes 'polyvalent' at once so evocative and so pleasing a word. Nothing short of trying to keep abreast of all that is going on in the world of industry and, in the light of this, planning for what lies ahead, can enable us to prepare our young people to live constructive, satisfying and happy lives. Even the worker of lowest skill must know more than is immediately required for his job, so that, in the words of M. Matray, a French writer on technical education, he 'completely dominates his craft'.

Examinations

The greatest obstacle to preparing young people to understand the world in which they are growing up, to be able to dominate their craft or professional skill, and to be able to contribute to the building of the harmonious co-operating world, longed for by every normal man and woman, is the nature of the traditional written examination.

So far as this country is concerned, the examination through which a stranglehold on almost all secondary education has been established is that now known as the 'General Certificate of Education' at its various levels. To trace rapidly how this situation has developed we must stress how, in the first two decades of this century, when there were always more workers than jobs, many groups of employers who needed clerical workers used the matriculation qualification of London University as a yardstick. Even when the more suitable 'School Certificate' had been introduced as an examination for all Grammar Schools, many banks and insurance offices valued more highly the five-subject Matriculation Exemption than passes in eight or nine subjects in School Certificate. So there arose a tendency to reduce the range of studies to assist youngsters in the competition for jobs, especially during the 'love-on-the-dole' years of the inter-war period.

In short, those who controlled industry and commerce also, in effect, controlled the nature of secondary education: he who paid the piper called the tune. There was probably nothing deliberate in this; it is doubtful if the Federation of British Industries, or any similar grouping of employers, ever discussed the curriculum of the Grammar Schools. There was certainly no malevolence and no desire to trammel education, and few of us were aware of the slow crystallization that was going on. But, with unemployment eating the very vitals of the manual worker, the competition for white collar jobs for their youngsters grew keener; bankruptcies might put toolmakers into the labour queue but they provided work for *clerks*. So the demand for preparation for the technical examinations of the City and Guilds of London Institute fell away; skill of hand and eye, even if combined with muscular strength, were at a discount: what was valued was the ability to regurgitate facts upon paper.

It hardly mattered what the facts were—the conditions of the Treaty of Utrecht, the difference between metaphors and metonyms, the sum of the exterior angles of a polygon, the use of 'ut' with the subjunctive case in Latin, 'where is the pen of my aunt' (in French), or the journeys of St. Paul; with the right five credits in School Certificate you could perhaps get a job in the Eastminster Bank and so be secure for life. For, however bad the unemployment, somehow the banks went on.

These were not years in which to look into the syllabuses of the examination, to ask oneself whether national history was sufficient preparation for living in a troubled world, or whether an ability to understand one's mother tongue and to write it clearly and simply was more important than a knowledge of the technical terms invented for its analysis by professional scholars. These were the times in which, though the most important provision of the 1918 Education Act (that creating Day Continuation Schools, which would have helped so much to keep young unemployed usefully occupied) was still unfulfilled, education was being cut left, right and centre. Teachers' salaries were reduced, fewer free places became available in Grammar Schools, school building almost ceased, 120 graduates were available for every vacant teaching post: if you were lucky enough to have a job in a Grammar School the only thing that mattered was to get the youngsters through their School Certificate with the highest marks they could get, often thanks to spotting some likely questions and making them learn up a lot of model answers.

And when the Spens Report appeared in 1938, with its superb analysis of the physical and psychological needs of adolescents, and with its visionary picture of the curriculum and its functions in a secondary school, it was already too late. The inability of those who had governed the country for so long to understand the forces which were changing the world had resulted in Hitler obtaining power in a country desperate with 7 millions of unemployed. Now Nemesis had risen and, in 1938, schools were busy planning 'evacuation' or 'reception' as the case might be. In vain did the Committee put into italics on p. 256 the following words regarding the School Certificate: '*we hold that in several important respects the influence of the examination and the process of preparation for it are inimical at present to the healthy growth in mind and body of a large number of children who pass through the Grammar School*': there were no ears to hear; we were listening to the Horst Wessel song.

If the words of the Spens Report were true in 1938, when the pass mark in every subject was about 35 per cent and the examination confined to Grammar Schools, how much more true must they be today, when the pass mark is approximately 50 per cent and thousands of less academic children in Secondary Modern Schools are being crammed to try to score a pass in two or three subjects?

Unfortunately the administratively awkward ideas put forward by the Spens Report were quietly put to rest by the Norwood Report of 1943. Here are the passages, once famous and now notorious, which gave their blessing to the tripartite system and left their baleful mark upon English education, as referred to in an earlier chapter.

The evolution of education has in fact thrown up certain groups, each of which can and must be treated in a way appropriate to itself.[7]

Here is a description of the first group:

English education has in practice recognised the pupil who is interested in learning for its own sake, who can grasp an argument or follow a piece of collected reasoning, who is interested in causes, whether on the level of human volition or in the material world, who cares to know how things came to be as well as how they are, who is sensitive to language as expression of thought . . . he is interested in the relatedness of related things, in development, in structure, in a coherent body of knowledge.[8]

This, of course, describes the boys who obtained their Matriculation Exemption and became bank clerks.

The second type of child is described thus:

He often has an uncanny insight into the intricacies of mechanism whereas the subtleties of language construction are too delicate for him. To justify itself to his mind, knowledge must be capable of immediate application, and the knowledge and its application which most appeal to him are concerned with the control of material things.[9]

He is the born motor mechanic.

Then, perhaps with Platonic eye upon the 'little bald tinker, who has come into money and has just had his chains knocked off, had a bath . . .'[10] the commissioners recognized the third group:

The pupil in this group deals more easily with concrete things than with ideas. He may have much ability, but it will be in the realm of facts. He is interested in things as they are; he finds little interest in the past or in the slow disentanglement of causes or movements. His mind must turn its knowledge or its curiosity to immediate test; and his test is essentially practical.[11]

So the Divine Providence created man not in one image but in three, one for the English Grammar School, one for the Secondary Technical School and one (perhaps many more than one) for the Secondary Modern School.

Still following the Platonic line the Committee say:

In a wise economy of secondary education, pupils of a particular type of mind would receive the training best suited to them and that training would lead them to an occupation where their capacities would be suitably used.[12]

Perhaps it is unkind to members of the Committee, but the resemblance is so striking that we must now quote from Lindsay's translation of Plato's Republic the passage in which

Socrates is explaining to Glaucon how his three different groups of society are to live happily together:

> You in this city are all brothers, so we shall tell our tale to them, but God, as he was fashioning you, put gold in those of you who are capable of ruling . . . he put silver in the auxiliaries, and iron and copper in the farmers and the other craftsmen.

Unfortunately, for a year or two the Norwood Report had considerable effect and it was during this time that the Secondary Schools Examination Council revised the nature of the School Certificate Examination with its 'groups' (languages, mathematics, the sciences and the English subjects), and instituted the General Certificate of Education as a 'subject' examination, in which no virtue is attached to having a broad education including representatives of even three of the former groups.[13]

Moreover, so as to make much more difficult the broad spread of subjects, and, it would seem, deliberately to encourage specialization, the pass mark was raised from approximately 35 per cent to approximately 50 per cent. The actual words of the report are:

> We envisage that a pass should have real significance—more, for instance, than has been implied by a 'Pass' in the School Certificate Examination. We should expect that the appropriate standard would in due course approximate more to what has been a 'Credit' standard in School Certificate.

There was an outcry from some of the schools, but it was of no avail: the recommendations were adopted by all the University Examining Boards. The writer has never been able to understand the motives that led to this change except by imputing to the Secondary Schools Examination Board of that time a desire to support the recommendations of the Norwood Committee. The words already quoted: 'In a wise economy of secondary education, pupils of a particular type of mind would receive the training best suited to them' would justify any attempt to prevent the children with iron and copper in them preparing for the School Certificate Examination. Whilst the pass mark was 35 per cent the situation might be tempting to the brighter of these pupils: raise it to 50 per cent and the prospect becomes firmly off-putting.

Unfortunately for the Platonists, the pressures towards democratization could not be held back, especially with Labour in control of the London County Council and some other industrial areas. So now, as a consequence of the construction of the General Certificate of Education, Ordinary Level, as a subject examination, thousands of youngsters who might have had a broad education and passed the old School Certificate in six or seven subjects, especially if the syllabus had been made more relevant to life, struggle hard indeed to wrest the meagre and perhaps sterile success of G.C.E. in three subjects, in two subjects, or even in one.

At the same time there has been a corresponding narrowing of pre-University studies. Whereas, thirty years ago, a boy preparing to read science at a university would have taken at least three subjects, say Chemistry, Physics and Maths, in Higher School Certificate, now in some Universities only two subjects at 'A' level are required, but the mark obtained must be high. For instance a young woman was recently informed by the Registrar of a certain University that she would be offered a place provided that she obtained over 65 per cent of marks in two given subjects at 'A' level. Naturally she neglected all other studies in the attempt to achieve this. Universities vary in their 'A' level requirements and within a given University there may be variation from Faculty to Faculty. But, to anyone who believes that young people entering a University should have a broad background, the summary of University Entrance requirements published by the National Union of Teachers makes sad reading.

Nor do the new regulations that come into force from December 31st, 1963 for the Universities of Manchester, Liverpool, Leeds, Sheffield and Birmingham offer any substantial improvement. But it is to be hoped that the encouragement there given for General Studies, even though it will be an examination subject, may result in broadening of the Sixth Form curriculum.

The disadvantages of this narrow specialization have been made clear by many people, but Sir Charles Snow in the Rede Lecture of 1959, 'The Two Cultures', brought things to a head. Attempts at reform have been put forward with vigour by A. D. C. Peterson[14] and through the A.B.C. group of Heads. No attempt, therefore, will be made here to pursue this subject further. But it must be hoped that some return to broader studies in the Sixth Form will soon be achieved.

Other examinations in secondary schools

We need, however, to consider further the plight of the Secondary Modern Schools and of the equivalent streams in Comprehensive Schools, vis-a-vis examinations, and to discover what are the causes that have brought these youngsters fully into the arena of the written examination.

First of all we must note that the 1944 Education Act provided not only for the raising of the school-leaving age but also for the creation of County Colleges. Indeed these latter were envisaged as having great urgency, for Section 43 states that

> On and after such dates . . . not later than three years after the date of commencement of this Part of the Act, it shall be the duty of every local education authority to establish and maintain county colleges, that is to say, centres approved by the Minister for providing for young persons who are not in full-time attendance at any school or other educational institution such further education, including physical practical and vocational training, as will enable them to develop their various aptitudes and capacities and will prepare them for the responsibilities of citizenship.

Had this section of the Act been implemented, the raising of the school-leaving age to 15 would have been seen as part of a continuous process of learning, for everybody, to the age of 18 at least. Moreover, the specific reference to the responsibilities of citizenship was a challenge to the County Colleges to develop studies which would have living contact with all aspects of community life, with visits to social enterprises, ranging from sewage farms to homes for aged people. Such civic studies have always formed part of the day release courses in the *Berufsschulen* which have been compulsory in Germany for all young workers under 18 ever since 1920. They give relevance to many other more academic studies and render them palatable.

But without the County Colleges ahead the Secondary Modern Schools had to look for some sort of objective at the end of the period of schooling and, unfortunately, such is the disproportionate esteem in which this regurgitative examination is held, it was to this that many teachers looked to provide the motivation to pupils not only for studying but for staying on at school after the age of 15.

It must be admitted, however, that another important factor in this drift to the G.C.E. was the failure, by and large, of the rank and file of the teachers in Secondary Modern Schools to rise to their opportunities. As the Spens Report shows, many teachers in pre-war Grammar Schools felt themselves prevented from being educators by the restrictive pressure of the examination syllabuses. They would have given much to have the opportunities of the teachers in Secondary Modern Schools when the school-leaving age was raised. Then was the glorious opportunity to plan a curriculum designed to help achieve what one conceived to be the main objectives in education. Most people will agree that these objectives include, in addition to loftier aims:

(*a*) some understanding of the society in which the pupils are growing up and its demands and its problems;

(*b*) some background knowledge which later may help in understanding to some extent a few of the scientific, political and economic problems of humanity as a whole;

(*c*) the ability to find information from books of reference and other reliable sources;

(*d*) enjoyment of the art of studying whatever it is that one wants to study, whether it be rabbit-keeping or motor cars;

(e) some experience in the application of critical thought to the ideas and values put over by the mass media—Press, film, radio and television.

If we accept these as important objectives in secondary education and reflect upon one's methods of achieving them, it becomes clear that the degree of success in such work can never be assessed by written examination. Indeed, the more relevant the education is to the personal life, health and happiness of the educand, the less is it adapted to being assessed by any examining authority.

If, therefore, the majority of teachers in Secondary Modern Schools and streams had held their objectives clearly before their eyes and had possessed enough expertise to devise ways of achieving them, they would not have sought to fetter themselves with external examinations. But they should not bear the blame alone: almost everyone concerned with policy and administration must share the blame, including the Inspectorate. In those immediate post-war years, too, everyone had too much to do, there was no time to think. Still worse, no provision was made or is made for giving anyone in the field of education any time to think. There are no sabbatical terms for young creative minds whether they be those of teachers, headmasters or any kind of administrator.[15] Even in our universities, where committee activities and other work of administration tend to absorb more and more time of senior members of teaching staff, a sabbatical term is a rare thing. If funds were made available for our universities to adopt the system of American universities of giving a regular sabbatical year, we might hope that the principle of sabbatical terms could be introduced for all kinds of educational administrators, so that they might have time to get things into perspective and to think.

Meanwhile our secondary schools are pushed around, first in this direction and then in that, by forces which are often irrelevant to the whole purpose of education. And, as we have seen, every now and then, when the interplay of irrelevant forces has produced an urgent problem which should have been seen afar off, the snap judgement is obtained of a hastily assembled

7

mixed committee of laymen and experts, all already over-occupied with other tasks.

Such was the Beloe Report, which has led to the development of the Certificate of Secondary Education, that is going to shackle the curriculum and the syllabuses of our Secondary Modern Schools and our Modern streams in other secondary schools. So the unsatisfactory situation all round, with regard to all written examinations of the G.C.E. type, throws into prominence the need for a long and deep consideration of this basic question:

Bearing in mind the ultimate aims of education, what should be the function and nature of school examinations?

Because of the immense changes, since school examinations were introduced, in the possibilities for all citizens of the British Isles, not only in physical standards of living but in opportunities through radio and television in having access to all that is best in human culture, we should expect the answers to this question to be very different from what in fact obtains today.

Now that no one any longer asks the question, 'Who shall be educated?', now that it is apparent that only through life-long education can humanity be enabled to handle with safety the continually increasing control over the forces of Nature which scientists of all nations are establishing, the function of examinations as a means of deciding who shall be taken and who shall be left is no longer significant. On the other hand, in a world where skills in control of machines are very important, practical examinations as tests of competence and reliability are likely to be increasingly important. Still more, in all work concerned with human beings, whether in nursing, medicine, teaching, in all forms of personnel work, foremanship and management, indeed perhaps even in political life, we must expect practical tests and assessments of competence to play an increasing part. Of course there will have to be studies and experiments in devising suitable tests and in making fair assessments, but much of this kind of thing has already been done in the field of technical education in this country and still more in Germany, Sweden and France. So adaptation of satisfactory techniques should not be too difficult.

But below the level of tests of competence we must surely expect such new types of examination as may be invented to have, as their main object, the discovery and recognition of a wide range of potentialities so that the examinee can be helped to decide upon the next step in his education or professional advancement. Put briefly, the function of examinations will be to facilitate individual fulfilment in paths that, in Godwin's words, generate happiness. Incidentally, the happiness of the individual himself will be promoted in the process. It is rather surprising that although any school may submit syllabuses to Examining Boards as alternatives, very few have ever done so.

This conception of the function of examinations, though it will seem strange at present, is not new. Ideas on the same lines were put forward by Sir Griffith Williams, K.B.E., C.B., in a paper read to the Royal Society of Arts of 1956. His subject was 'Examinations: do we still need them?' After a wide review of past and present Sir Griffith concluded with the following words:

> Do we still need examinations? The answer is 'Yes', but to a greatly diminished extent, since the expansion of our educational system is making competition unnecessary and out of date. The function of examinations in the future will be to fit the right pegs into the right holes and for this purpose written examinations by themselves are a poor instrument. We have yet to find the right technique, but we may assume that it will include these elements:
>
> (i) a qualifying test in writing or otherwise;
> (ii) a personal interview;
> (iii) a report of previous progress by the candidates' own teachers.
>
> How exactly these three elements are to be combined one cannot at present say. Very probably they will vary according to the purpose of the examination and the age of the candidate. But a great deal of research will be needed before we can be said to have mastered the subject and found a solution. At present we are like Alice and the Cheshire Cat.[16]

It is not surprising that we are far from a solution. Firstly, there is no permanent solution in a world of change, still less in a world of accelerating change such as that of today. But, even more important, we cannot adapt the function of examinations to the changed conditions of today until we have adapted our methods of education; most important of all, until we have clearly defined, or re-defined, our aims.

CHAPTER EIGHT

New Aims and New Methods in Secondary Education

GODWIN's definition of the aim of education as 'the genera- tion of happiness' is broad enough to stand for a fairly long span of time. Succeeding periods will introduce fresh circumstances and fresh climates of thought on religious, social and economic and political questions, but 'the generation of happiness' will remain a worth-while aim even though there will be new ways of striving to attain this simple but clear ideal.

If one puts oneself, so to speak, into an intellectual space capsule, spinning like cosmonauts round and round the world, looking down in a detached way upon all the political and social systems of the earth, one surely arrives at an analysis something like the following. It is intended as a synoptic view of what, directly or indirectly, consciously or unconsciously, the nations of the world are striving to achieve:

(a) nationally a democratic (variously defined), co-operating community capable of using increasing leisure for the advancement of happiness;

(b) internationally, a co-operating world possessing unlimited resources revealed by science;

these two developments permitting (with certain obvious exceptions) the fullest possible development, material and spiritual, of every being, whatever his colour, race or creed.

Behind all the smoke screens of capitalism and communism these things, it would appear, do all the nations of the world seek after.

If, then, it is for these things that the hearts of men and women all over the world are longing, even though they at present see different routes for achieving them, surely education for the generation of happiness in the last third of the twentieth century must incidentally seek to promote these specific objectives.

If this argument be accepted, we have a series of very useful touchstones which can be applied both to the elements of the school curriculum and to the methods of education. All studies and methods which promote the development of a democratic co-operating community, the beneficial use of leisure and some advance towards a co-operating world should be encouraged; any that would work in the opposite directions should be restricted or abandoned.

There is, however, one other overriding consideration which must also be used as a touchstone in every case—does the subject and/or method promote the ideal of life-long education?

Motivation for life-long education

We have already seen how the changes that lie ahead in economic and social life are such that most men and women must expect continually to be learning new tasks as a means of earning their living or even running their homes and bringing up their children. In the words of Norman Cousins, Editor of America's important journal for the intelligentsia, *The Saturday Review*:

> No man can claim to be well educated unless he regards knowledge as a living thing, requiring constant nourishment for vital growth. This holds true of his profession or occupation or his thinking about the world itself and his place in it.

With the enormous changes of material outlook which follow upon economic unions between groups of nations there arise corresponding demands for change in political and cultural outlooks among the whole people, whether it is a community with democratic voting powers or not. Life-long education, even if not very formal education, thus becomes an essential part of life for everyone. But this cannot take place as it should if the years of compulsory schooling do not leave in the minds of the educands a memory of hours of stimulus, of mental occupation which was delightful, even if sometimes it was strenuous, and a belief in the powers of reason as a means of reducing human suffering, promoting human welfare, easing the tensions between groups of individuals and, in effect, even if the words would not be acceptable to all, advancing the Kingdom of Heaven upon earth.

So it is far more important that adolescents should leave school ignorant but keen to know; healthy and with a delight in the use of their bodies, capable of enjoying music and all the arts, kindly and co-operative with their peers, than that they should leave school crammed with information, physically and culturally 'illiterate' (as so many French *lycéens* emerge from their schools), selfishly competitive and conceited. In the words of Jean-Jacques Rousseau:

> It is very strange that ever since people began to think about education they should have hit upon no other way of guiding children than emulation, jealousy, envy, vanity, greediness, base cowardice, all the most dangerous passions, passions ever ready to ferment, ever prepared to corrupt the soul even before the body is full grown.

Horace Mann, more than a century later, echoes the same idea:

> Of emulation in school as an incitement to effort I can here say but a word . . . let those who use it as a quickener of the intellect beware, lest it prove a depraver of the social affections. . . . No cruelty towards a child can be so great as that which barters morals for attainment.

But over a great part of the world the cult of the written examination holds sway and the words of Rousseau or Horace Mann or of others who think like them are seldom heard.

Western capitalist society is ruthlessly competitive until it reaches the size when takeover bids no longer have any meaning. The same spirit of competition saturates much of English education. Grammar Schools and Public Schools vie with one another in the battle for open scholarships at Oxford and Cambridge. At a lower level secondary Headmasters and Headmistresses (but fortunately not the best of them) annually offer the number, or percentage, of examination successes as proof of their successful stewardship. Unfortunately, the thoughtless majority of the general public take this as an adequate criterion of the school's work.

Nor are the schools which offer grammar-type education in Germany or France one whit better in this respect than any secondary schools in England; indeed, especially in France, they are far worse.

It must be clear, however, that so long as the copingstone to almost every course of study at school is some form of written examination, with its associated spirit of competition, it is going to be very difficult indeed to produce a population in which the majority of people are going to regard learning as a life-long process. What is more, the idea of fairness, which is one of the few good assumptions inherent in the examination process, in the end prevents individuals from pursuing different lines of study. With the best will in the world it is difficult to establish exact equivalence between examination papers in different subjects. So in certain fields of work, restricted at first until satisfactory techniques have been evolved, we should openly admit that the writ of exact equivalence no longer runs, that competition should no longer take place, that one star differeth from another in glory, and that success is to be measured not in examination marks, but in the personal satisfaction and happiness of the worker in what he has produced and, perhaps, though to a smaller extent, in the approbation of his tutor.

Relevance as motivation for learning

In addition to freedom to follow one's own interests there is another factor which is of great power in providing motivation for adolescent study and this is—relevance. Far too much intellectual material which young people are expected to master has no relevance to the next twenty years of their lives, and may never have the slightest effect, except as a mental encumbrance. The philosopher Maritain has called it 'damp wood': A. N. Whitehead referred to it as 'inert ideas'. Everyone who is honest with himself, and puts aside that feeling of protectiveness and affection that one feels for anything which one possesses, whether it be a dog or an item of knowledge, will admit that the curriculum of most secondary schools is rich with junk. And so, for reasons largely beyond their control, and which will be discussed in a later chapter, are the minds of many of the older teachers; and so, because school finances are too limited to change the textbooks frequently, are many of the textbooks. Only a year or two ago I found a class of 13-year-old boys, in a highly respected London Grammar School, being set to copy from a Geography textbook drawings of the Yurts in which the inhabitants of a certain part of the U.S.S.R. were depicted as living. Actually the region had for a decade or so been one of mushrooming modern towns and collective farms. And the textbook, which was still being printed and selling widely, bore a title redolent with up-to-dateness.

The fact is that, for many studies which must be kept up to date, the present textbook system is completely unsatisfactory. Publishers vie with one another to produce books which are largely designed to fit examination syllabuses and which are produced as cheaply as possible, so far as cheapness is compatible with readability for the victim. For so long as the textbook allowance of most secondary schools is so limited that they must consider very carefully whether one book costs a shilling less than another, though the dearer one, by virtue of its illustrations and size of print, is much more attractive to the reader, so long will enjoyment of the learning process, and the up-to-dateness of the material, be restricted. In the U.S.S.R. and other communist countries, where textbooks are produced centrally by the million, it is possible to revise text books annually if necessary. This in actual fact may not happen, errors may be perpetuated and there are no rivals; indeed, inconvenience would be caused if there were. But in this country the cut-throat competition between publishers makes them inevitably reluctant to scrap a book which is selling reasonably well. Whilst I would actively oppose the introduction of the Soviet system, since it provides a method of thought control, I consider that both some agreement among publishers regarding the sections of the educational field that they will exploit, and a considerable increase in the sums allowed for school textbooks by Local Education Authorities are extremely desirable.

Even so, the relatively new educative media—film, radio and television, have a much greater part to play than they play at present. They can provide up-to-dateness such as no textbook can offer and television lessons in geography can, at their best, be almost as realistic as personal experience.

It is important to consider the factors which have restricted the growth and use of radio and television in secondary schools.

There are, of course, first of all, the public examinations. Everyone who has ever prepared young people for public examinations knows that there are certain guiding rules which, within limits, should be observed in examination classes if one wants to achieve the highest degree of success for the highest proportion of pupils in the class. These include:

(1) Cover the whole syllabus if possible but do not waste time introducing extraneous matter: even if you do, for the good of the pupils' souls, they will resent your action and their souls will become even blacker as a result of their resentment.

There are certain things which all examiners will expect the pupils to know: make certain that they know these and can reproduce them quickly by giving them frequent drill.

(2) Give frequent short tests not only to check the pupils' knowledge but to train them continually to work against time. Mark the papers at home: there is no time for discussion. Remember that examinations are not a test of what a youngster *knows* but how much of what he knows he *can write down* in a given space of time.

(3) Study the back papers for the last ten years. If you make out an analysis on a large sheet you may be able to spot one or two questions in every paper. Provide mimeographed model answers for ten possible questions and get them learned.

These are, of course, only the most elementary tips in the game of teacher versus examiner. The champion teachers have, in addition, a vast amount of esoteric expertise which they reveal only to their closest friends, or perhaps not even to them.

It is apparent from the foregoing that radio or television lessons, or fine scientific films, or anything relevant to life but outside the examination syllabus, would be worse than a waste of the time of the pupils: it would constitute deliberate sabotage and be an offence against the Governors of the school, the head, the parents and the unfortunate child. As teachers are among the most honourable of all professional workers, such sabotage never takes place: at least I have never heard of such a thing happening in a form of youngsters preparing for an examination.

Whilst at stages earlier than the examination year it should, theoretically, be possible to use mass media without transgressing the canons of professional responsibility, we must point out that preparation for an examination is not something confined to one year: unless the syllabus outlined for all the previous years has been covered the pupil in the examination year will be severely handicapped. So, especially in those Grammar Schools where competition for University entrance is at present so important an issue that pupils must, to succeed, spend three years in the Sixth Form (and accordingly must previously cover in three, or at most four, years a syllabus originally planned for a five-year course), in practice *all* classes are working against time and under the exigencies of the syllabus drawn up by the teacher in charge of the subject.

There is not, therefore, much place for lessons by radio or television or film in the majority of Grammar Schools.

Mass media in education versus school buildings

But even when teachers desire to use these things, there are all sorts of physical obstacles to be overcome: in the case of a film it must arrive on the right day, one must have a skilled operator for the projector and one must have the use of the room that can be darkened, and one must have it for the right time-table period of the day. And even then, as all rooms, except the hall, even science lecture rooms if any, are built to hold about thirty-five pupils one cannot save time, and justify all the trouble, by showing the film at one fell swoop to three parallel forms, and so on. What is more, it is a hoary, outworn, absurd tradition that implies that large groups of adolescents cannot be occupied quietly together by suitable films or radio or television broadcasts. In short, schools have not been built in such a way as to facilitate the use of modern teaching instruments and at the same time to economize in the use of teachers. Nor, owing to the rigid financial restrictions imposed by the Treasury through the Ministry of Education, is it possible for Authorities to experiment in the building of schools with rooms, additional to normal classrooms, which can be used for the accommodation of groups larger than a normal form for radio, television or film lessons.

In July 1962 Mr. A. L. Hutchinson, County Education Officer for the Isle of Wight, in his presidential address to the Association of Education Officers, speaking of post-war school building, said:

> It may well be that the final verdict of a Pevsner of the twenty-first century will be that we have lost our golden opportunities....[1]

Far too often price control has dictated an 'unenviable choice between the size of different rooms so that one has to be smaller than it should be to enable the other to function effectively'. We must contrast this with the situation in the United States where in 1959 the National Association of Secondary School Principals produced, as the result of the work of an Experimental Study Commission, two brilliantly concise reports, 'Images of the Future' and 'New Directions to Quality Education'.

Here are a few extracts from the former:

> The secondary school of the future will not have standard classes of 25 to 35 pupils meeting five days a week on inflexible schedules. Both the size of the groups and the length of the classes will vary

from day to day. Methods of teaching, student groupings, and teacher and pupil activities will adjust to the purpose and content of instruction.

No longer will one teacher endeavor to be in charge of all of a class's activities in one subject. Instead teaching will be organised to be more efficient and effective.

Some aspects of learning will be presented by specially qualified teachers to relatively large groups of students. This, in turn, will provide more opportunities for students to explore ideas in small discussion groups. Although some classes will be much larger, paradoxically the student will assume more individual responsibility for learning.

The school will be organised around three kinds of activities:

Large-group Instruction   Individual Study
Small-group Discussion

Large-group Instruction

Large-group instruction will include a number of activities carried out in groups of 100 or more students. Instruction will be by teachers who are particularly competent, who have more time to prepare, and who will utilise the best possible instructional aids. . . .

These large-group activities will occupy about 40 per cent of the students' time. The amount of time spent in large groups will vary according to subjects, at different stages within a subject and in accordance with student interest and maturity.

Individual Study

Students will engage in *study* activities as individuals, or in groups of two or three, with a minimum of constant supervision.

Study activities will require students progressively to take more responsibility for self-direction. The amount of time will vary according to subject and student maturity. On an average it will be about 40 per cent of their time.

Small-group Discussion

Small groups of 12 to 15 students and a teacher will pit mind against mind to sharpen understanding. They will examine terms and concepts, solve problems, and reach areas of agreement and disagreement. . . . The *discussion* activities will occupy about 20 per cent of the students' time.

The class of 25 to 35—so frequently found in today's schools, and often highly esteemed—will have no regular place in the secondary school of tomorrow. A class of 25 is unnecessarily small for *large-group instruction* activities . . . too large for effective *study* . . . too large for successful *discussion*. Research in group process indicates that a group cannot be larger than 12 to 15 if there is to be effective participation of all its members.

And here is an extract from 'New Directions to Quality Education':

Staff Patterns

Employ the following staff pattern for a school of 400 students, or for each 400 students in a larger school—

10 Professional Teachers working full time.

Instruction Assistants for 200 hours per week.

Clerical Assistants for 100 hours per week.

General Aides for 50 hours per week.

Community Consultants and Staff Specialists as needed.

(This does not include administrative-supervisory personnel and their assistants.)

Assign professional teachers in accordance with the competences and interests of each.

Allocate specific parts of the teaching job to Instruction Assistants.

(They will be mostly part-time workers selected on the bases of training and experience. Such persons might be housewives well trained in subject areas, former teachers, and teacher education students attending higher institutions.)

Employ General Aides for non-specialised tasks and other persons for clerical duties.

Establish a file of qualified Community Consultants to be available to present specialised material.

The National Association of Secondary School Principals received financial help from the Ford Foundation to enable the Experimental Study Commission to perform its work. Perhaps there could be no more laudable project for support by one of the British charitable Foundations than an investigation of similar character.

It is clear that if a report on similar lines were to result, we should have to change the views of the Ministry with regard to school buildings, of the Government with regard to educational T.V. and to the production of teaching films by the Schools Department of the B.B.C., and of the teachers in secondary schools with regard to the nature of their job. But first we should have to change the nature of the public examination papers which we set to our secondary school pupils. And that would not be a bad thing, either!

Meanwhile, in the United Kingdom inadequate use can be made of the mass media, though large-group instruction by living teachers on the American plan could still be used if only the school buildings were so constructed to permit variable sizes of groups.

Since it is so largely the examination syllabuses which prevent widespread educational use of the mass media, we would have expected that in the Secondary Modern Schools they would be used to a considerable extent. But the physical difficulties which hamper the Grammar Schools apply at least as much to the Secondary Modern Schools. And, whereas a Grammar School may have a laboratory technician who can operate the film projector for any teacher who wishes to use it, few Secondary Modern Schools have a laboratory technician and very many have no laboratory at all. Indeed, the enquiry reported by the Science Masters Association at the end of 1960 revealed that less than half of the Secondary Modern Schools in England and Wales have properly equipped laboratories and that in some schools no science at all is taught. Moreover, of those schools where science is taught, over 40 per cent have to teach it to groups of more than thirty children. For contrast we might remind ourselves that in all subjects in which practical work is involved in Sweden no class is allowed to exceed fifteen pupils.

We can summarize the position regarding (a) the economies that could be made in teaching power, and (b) the greater interest and relevance that could be given to school studies by modern media, by saying that the present Ministry policy with regard to the building of secondary schools and the low figure per place which is permitted (£310 in 1962) make any substantial advance in these directions impossible.

Study-halls, libraries and reading rooms

There is another way, even more important, though less capable of early adoption, by which young people could be put upon the path of life-long learning and this is by the provision of what in the U.S.A. are called 'study-halls'. At present, in our good primary schools, quite small children learn how to use little books of reference, taking them from the class library, making their abstract, returning the book to its place and so on. All over the country one may find primary classes engaged in this sort of purposeful activity, moving around the room quietly and with splendid self-control; behaving, in fact, in many cases, like little adults. And they are clearly enjoying their little books with the bright pictures.

But when they reach the average secondary school the situation is different. The unfortunate division of the studies into rigid subjects, each to be pursued to some depth, makes the provision of a satisfactory form library quite impossible. As for the school library, in a school of 400 it can usually hold only one class at a time. Indeed, in the past few years, schools to hold 700 or even 1,000 secondary pupils have been built with library space for only 35 pupils. And the reason has been the Ministry's financial limit per pupil place. The Local Education Authority had had to choose between having a small library and several laboratories and a large library but no laboratories and had rightly made the former choice. But this was a dilemma which they should not have had to face. The Treasury's penny-wise policy is bound to be particularly foolish with regard to education, which must always be regarded as long-term investment which will bring high capital appreciation. But, unfortunately, ever since the ruthless Geddes axe was applied to education in 1927, economizing in education has been, with few and short interludes, the policy of successive Governments, with British economic importance declining steadily as the cumulative result of the educational parsimony.

So school study-halls, where youngsters can learn to work on their own, or school libraries big enough to contain one fifth of the school at a time, are virtually non-existent in the state-aided system of education. Yet life-long learning, whether liberal or vocational, cannot be established before the habit of using books, and of enjoying using them, has been formed. It has often been said, but no truth is lost in the repetition, that what matters more than memorized knowledge is knowing where to find the information that one needs. In a world where the agents of thought-control and the hidden persuaders are increasing their power perhaps in every country, it is more necessary than it ever has been in the past that our young people should learn how to check statements made in mass media against reliable sources of printed information. They are only likely to learn to do this in the critical intellectual atmosphere provided by a place of learning, so they need to have the sources of reference handy in such a place and to have plenty of practice in using them.

Following this line of thought it also becomes clear that every secondary school should have a large newspaper reading room in which newspapers of every political complexion should be represented, as these provide the daily material upon which critical thought needs continually to be exercised. Even so, the newspapers of one nation are not enough provision for any secondary school today. English secondary schools should have also good representative weekly newspapers from the U.S.A. and Canada, from Ghana and Nigeria, and so on, and at least one daily newspaper from each of the countries of which the languages are being studied in the school.

All this, of course, needs more floor space, but floor space is easier to provide than teachers and its maintenance is far less costly. The disease from which day Grammar Schools suffer most at the present time is chalk and talk teaching. The real function of a secondary school at this stage of human advancement is not to teach, but to enable young people to learn. It is true that most young people will need guiding in this

8

process and that in order to form high standards they will need to meet some of the best things in music, in art, in literature; to hear about some of the noblest lives of men and women and to be conversant with the ideals of the Christian and other religions.

But they do not need to be talked at by flesh and blood, and mentally exercised in groups of thirty or so, for seven consecutive periods a day. Indeed, if while they are being taught they are being *well* taught, they will do better to follow each lesson by a period of assimilation and follow-up than by having, as holds at present, to switch their minds immediately to some entirely different subject. No efficient adult arranges his activities in the kaleidoscopic form of a school timetable. The proper provision of space in library and study-halls would enable the pupils to do much more thinking, learning and personal work than at present, whilst in fact resting their nerves from the jangle of classroom procedures and refreshing themselves for new mental intake in subsequent periods. Even the youngest pupil in secondary school should have at least one period per day when he is working on his own in library or study-hall. As he grows older he should have more such periods, until he reaches the Sixth Form where, of course, even today, every pupil has private study periods. Our present error, forced upon us by economy in building costs, is that we generally limit such private study periods to the Sixth Form.

Academic helpers in schools

Of course, very young adolescents in the school library will need guidance, and one teacher-librarian on duty in a library where 150 young pupils are working may well be insufficient. It is here that we might well take a leaf out of the education book of the U.S.S.R. and invite retired teachers, ex-pupils who are at the University and other friends of the school, to promise regularly a few hours per week of help to individuals, and this is the form such help might best take in the United Kingdom. In the U.S.S.R. such helpers receive no remuneration or payment of travel expenses, but the pressures upon the individual to play his part in voluntary social work are adequate to supply the motivation. In England and Wales, where no such pressures exist, it would probably be right and proper to provide a small financial easement, such as would cover the cost of travel and meals and leave a little to spare.

Even if three or four such helpers were engaged with a group of 150 pupils it would be much cheaper than employing teachers and possibly even more effective, since the help of a disinterested person might be accepted with better grace. In any case there is everything to be gained and nothing to be lost by involving a greater number of persons in the work of education.

Indeed, such is going to be the increasing demand for secondary education that the nations will be hard put to it to spare enough of their most gifted men and women for the work. At the primary level, thanks to Nature's wise provision that about one half of all human beings should be female, gifted with the patience and sympathy needed for the bringing up of little children, there will always be enough potential teachers, provided, as we have seen, that married women who have brought up their little ones are enticed back into teaching. But at the secondary level the matter is quite different. The ability to study and to explain at a relatively advanced level, to give inspiration and leadership to adolescents full of energy and problems, is not found in a high proportion of the race. High intelligence and the capacity to teach a group of adolescents may, indeed, sometimes seem mutually exclusive.

In any case, if a much greater proportion of the population is to be engaged in secondary school teaching than at present, then either these people will be withdrawn from other walks of life where they may also be needed, or the intellectual quality of persons entering the profession will fall. It is no insult to young secondary school teachers of today to say that, in general, they have not the same intellectual ability as those entering the secondary teaching profession in the pre-war years. This is particularly the case with regard to mathematics and science, for the financial inducement to people who have the ability to obtain good qualifications in these subjects are far less in the teaching profession than in any other save the Church.

Teaching machines and language laboratories

The prospect for the future, therefore, is either a slow but steady fall in the standard of teaching in secondary schools or a better use of existing teaching of high quality. It has already been suggested that by a proper design of secondary school buildings the latter solution can be permitted and would be the better one. Moreover, still further aid is coming to the good teacher from programmed learning and the new teaching machines. Although teaching machines are at present only in their infancy, enough experimental work has been done to show that a very great deal of the drudgery of teaching can be effectively handed over to them. This will give the teacher both more time and more energy for those personal and pastoral relations which are the core of his job, those contacts in which he gives inspiration, opens up new lines of thought, extols examples of excellence or explains in a simple and clear way intricacies of thought in which the student has become bogged down.

In a similar way language laboratories have already transformed the outlook for the teaching of a wide range of language in secondary schools. The old system of a lesson during which any one pupil would be lucky if he were called upon to speak five words of the language in forty minutes will soon become a thing of the past—as language laboratories are now being installed in many Grammar Schools, Technical and Comprehensive Schools throughout the country.

All such mechanical aids can be of the greatest service to the community provided that those who control the purse strings of education believe in investment in human beings, and can see that it is better to spend on a lot of equipment and fewer good teachers than on a large number of mediocre teachers working on antiquated and inefficient lines.

We arrive, then, at quite a different conception of the nature of a secondary school building—or rather of what the Americans call the School Plant, since it may comprise an assortment of buildings. In particular the total superficial area will be far greater, so as to include a large library, study-hall, several projection rooms of different sizes and far more provision for the development of all kinds of manual skill.

It is also relevant to suggest that the existing system by which a Local Authority charges rates upon its own Education Committee, and then, of course, pays the rates should be abolished. This would reduce the anxiety that Councillors sometimes feel about superficial area in school buildings and at the same time economize in the clerical work involved in moving the papers from the right hand pocket of the Local Authorities to its left.

Hobby skills in boarding and day schools

Public boarding schools have for many decades, especially since the example of Sanderson of Oundle, provided splendid workshops in which any boys—however intellectual—could use some of their leisure in actually making things if they so desired. They could turn their minds from the abstract to the concrete, with gain to their nerves, their insight into mechanisms, their physical health and their happiness. Here is a list of some of the activities which have been provided by one quite small Public School of 270 boys: Woodwork, Metalwork, Engineering, Electronics, Glasswork, Model Aircraft, Model Railways, Pottery, Printing, Cinematography, Claymodelling, Photography, Forestry, Ornithology, Pond Microscopy, Meteorology, Gliding, Bookbinding, Car building. In addition there are Literary, Musical, Scientific, Debating, Poetry, Choral and Dramatic Societies.[2]

Day schools, however, by and large, lag behind in such provision unless it exists mainly for the use of those who are less academically inclined, and who will take subjects such as Woodwork, Metalwork and Machine-drawing as subjects in public examinations. Enough provision, however, should be made to enable *any* pupils, boys or girls, to understand, if they wish, the mechanisms of motor cars and perhaps other forms of machinery and also to make pots, or weave or develop some other manual skill.

This provision can often be arrived at in two ways—either by extending the number of workshops or, theoretically much easier, extending the number of hours during which the workshops may be used. This little corridor of an idea leads, in fact, into another which is, in fact, a vast cavern of an idea which has been developed by Mr. John Odesjo in Gothenburg, Sweden, in the last thirty years.

As a teacher of handicraft in wood and metal he conceived the idea of the school premises being opened for two or three hours every night for those children in the neighbourhood who desired to practise and extend their manual skills, whether in handicrafts, drawing and painting and woodcarving, or in cookery or in orchestral playing.

In the United Kingdom, in the best day secondary schools, many societies such as drama groups, choir, orchestra, fencing club, gramophone society and table-tennis club meet under the loose surveillance of a member of staff to pursue their laudable activities. No one would wish this system to cease. But, because parents are expecting their children home from school for a family meal, and because there is homework to be done, the extra-curricular activities tend to be a little overhung by the shadow of relentless time and the city bus services. In country schools to which most of the pupils come by special buses such after school extra-curricular activities naturally are almost non-existent.

The Gothenburg plan—which has long since spread into most cities of Sweden—uses the neighbourhood and not just the normal school population of the building, as the source of recruitment for evening activities. So this reduces travel and saves time and money for the youngsters.

For the younger children, whose homework will be finished early, activities may run from 5 p.m. till 7 p.m., it being remembered that the school day in Sweden ends by 3 p.m. having started at 8 a.m. Older age groups come from 6 p.m.

to 8 p.m. and from 7 p.m. to 9 p.m. and even from 8 p.m. to 10 p.m. The instructors *include* practising teachers who voluntarily undertake the extra work, but, in order to leave full-time teachers for their daily job, the evening instructors, as far as possible, are either retired teachers, married women formerly teachers, or practitioners of various arts and crafts who enjoy helping keen youngsters to cook, sew, weave, repair cars, build boats, paint pictures, make children's toys, furniture, decorated iron or copper work, pottery and so on. Each group is limited in size and is run as a club, the adult acting as leader. The club leader receives modest payment. There are no formal lessons but the leader helps the individual to make, within reasonable limits, whatever he wants to make. So we seldom see two youngsters having the same enterprise.

Putting school buildings to greater use

But beyond the obvious advantages of such a system lies the astonishing principle—that the school plant is not handed over, after school hours, for the 12 hours of slumber after cleaning which it would have in England: instead it is pressed into service till 10 p.m. in the interests of constructive and enjoyable leisure. Of course there are many school buildings in England which are used for Evening Institute classes, there are the Cambridgeshire Village Colleges which are schools by day and adult education centres of high quality by night, and there are school buildings serving similar functions in Oxfordshire and elsewhere. But, by and large, school buildings in this country, and especially the workshops, domestic science rooms and gymnasia, are not used as much as they *could* be used, or, indeed, *should* be used in view of their cost of building, equipment and maintenance. No modern business concern would allow expensive plant to function for a mere 30 hours out of 168 hours in every working week and also to rest unused for not less than twelve solid weeks per year. That is what we do in England and Wales.

In the United States during the summer vacation (admittedly

longer than in England and Wales) many schools open the
premises every morning just for games and library and cultural activities (*e.g.*, music and art) and all manual skills of
the woodwork, metalwork and home economics range, the
teachers who supervise receiving extra payment, of course.

But in this country the empty silence of educational institutions of all kinds for long periods is traditional and the caretaker
reigns over his domain in solitary, but very real, state; captain
of an empty stranded crewless ship, but captain all the same
and haughty monarch of all the emptiness he surveys.

It is time that the whole question of the proper use of educational buildings provided by public funds became the subject
of a Royal Commission. Probably nothing would result, but at
least the problem would have been recognized, or dragged
out of its hiding place and looked at. In my opinion the resident
caretaker would have to be supplemented by other male
full-time workers such as the janitors in American universities
and a good deal of the part-time female labour would thus be
displaced. But the additional costs would be nothing in comparison with the gain to the community resulting from a more
economic use of public buildings.

Of course, to begin with there would be the fear of teachers
that evening activities would damage their favourite tools,
break their domestic crockery, score the floor of the gymnasia
with scratches deep as tramlines and so on. But if this does not
happen in Sweden, why should it happen here?

Extending the time-table hours for senior pupils

Yet there is still another use, perhaps even more heretical a
suggestion, to which English state-aided secondary school
buildings might be put after 4 p.m.—lessons for the pupils,
especially for older ones. Anyone familiar with English Public
Schools for boys knows that in the winter months, in order that
daily open-air exercise shall be taken, the afternoon till 4 p.m.
is always free from lessons. Lessons are given on three or
four days per week from 4 p.m. till 5.30 p.m. or, it may be,
till 6 p.m. The system has worked well for a very long time:

no one ever complains about it, so it would seem that it brings advantages to all. Whilst there might be difficulties at first with city transport services if the system were to be introduced for all boys and girls over 14 years of age in city schools, these would probably be overcome by minor adjustments of bus timetables. So far as country secondary schools are concerned the solution might involve extra bus services, but again this would be a relatively small expenditure for a relatively large gain.

But the real argument for getting away from the idea that adolescents of 14 years and over cannot be expected to attend formal lessons after 4 p.m. is to make possible the more economic use of teaching staff. Just as a member of the teaching staff of a Technical College may do some of his teaching during the day and some during the evening, so there seems no reason (provided they are not given more than their due share, and the timetable is arranged to free them for long periods in the day), why teachers of senior forms should not do some of their work between 9 a.m. and 4 p.m. and the rest between 4 p.m. and 6 p.m. or between 6 p.m. and 8 p.m. Things like this, and others much more difficult, were willingly done by teachers of schools in evacuation during the Second World War.

This plan would have the following advantages:

(1) it would enable schools to utilize more help of part-time married women teachers during the middle hours of the day while their own children were at school;

(2) it would enable older pupils to get more open-air exercise: they would also do private study in library and study-halls during normal school hours, having some lessons after 4 p.m.

(3) in cities it would enable highly qualified Sixth Form teachers who are in short supply, e.g. in Maths and Science, to teach combined groups of pupils from a number of schools after normal school hours.

These pupils could come together from, say, 6 p.m. to 8 p.m. and for students of this age the extra travel would hardly matter. This applies also to subjects which are important but for which there is little demand. It is uneconomic to have a highly-qualified Sixth Form mistress teaching Russian to, say, three girls, when eight other girls of the same age and ten boys of the same age, scattered about the city in other schools, would dearly like the same opportunity, which their own schools cannot provide. In any case, the small Sixth Form groups are extremely expensive and if all the facts were publicly known about the small size of many Sixth Form groups, especially those being coached for Open Scholarships, there might well be an outcry. The foregoing suggestions illustrate a few possibilities which would result from a re-thinking of the whole business of the use of school premises. It is obviously important that the matter should be looked into from first principles by people whose minds are open on the matter. Perhaps an international group, including both Swedes and Americans, would be helpful in surveying this problem.

Education for independent thought

One of the responsibilities of schooling has always been to prepare the young person to find his way in the adult world. In a community which accepts, or at least pays lip service to, the ideal of individual responsibility, the liberty of conscience and so on, this must mean helping the child to live as an individual, with a mind of his own. So great, powerful, seductive and pervading have become the mass media that for most of us it is now probably far more difficult truly to have a mind of our own than it has been for a long time. We may flatter ourselves that our thoughts are our own, but if the material on which our thinking is done has already been astutely selected for us and pre-digested with emotional pepsin, the chances of our metabolizing individual thoughts are small indeed. Yet this, in fact, is the situation over a large part of the earth's surface today. In communist countries the control over thought processes is open and direct. In the U.S.A. the pre-digestion of information, and its discreet selection, is achieved with such skill that it is extremely difficult to recognize what is happening to one's mind. In even a few weeks of living in the

U.S.A., cut off from one's accustomed sources of critical comment and finding little in the U.S.A. to replace them, a European may find his thinking rapidly falling into the standard pattern on all sorts of economic and political issues.

The financial linkage between big business, Press, television, radio and film is such that information which would be detrimental to the bipolar doctrine of the supreme virtue of private enterprise and the wholly evil nature of socialism and communism is either quietly suppressed, or distorted, or, in effect, negated by the remarks of a respected commentator.

Many Americans in Universities are, of course, perturbed at the situation and at the failure of the schools to promote critical thinking.

In November 1962 a conference on the relation between civil liberty and the American educational system was sponsored by the American Political Science Association, the Association of American Law Schools, the National Council for Social Studies and the Civil Liberties Educational Foundations. The conference concluded that education in the principles of a free society 'is in a backwater, both in terms of the time committed to it, and the care and thought devoted to determining its method and content'. But the schools 'merely reflected the general social values that were now being honoured by Americans'.[3]

One would hazard a guess that in the U.S.A. nine people out of ten have their thought conditioned by mass media. In the United Kingdom, in spite of evidence submitted to the Pilkington Committee on the change in the values which can be attributed to the commercial motivation behind Independent Television, the proportion of people affected is probably somewhat lower. In the Scandinavian countries it is surely lower still and in France perhaps lowest of all.

One of the reasons for the difference lies in objectives in education. French education, more than any other, inherits the Hellenic ideals. It seeks, above all else, clarity of thought. Anyone who has been privileged to handle examination scripts written in the French baccalaureat examination and is familiar with scripts written in the 'A' level examination in England will know what a contrast there is in the way in which the answer is organized in France. Whereas in England, in G.C.E. examinations in which information is what the examiner is mainly seeking, bad arrangement of the fact will make little difference to the marks, in France a clear, logical and well ordered presentation of the material is essential for obtaining good marks, and reasoned arguments are considered extremely important. But the emphasis on clear thought, individualism and fierce educational competition in France is not without its drawbacks, for it does not promote social and political cohesion, as the history of the last century shows.

Nevertheless, in the world of mass control of opinion, France may in the end stand out as one of the last refuges of individualism.

Meanwhile, for us in the United Kingdom, there is still time to recognize the danger and to set out, in our secondary education, to develop a critical outlook among many of our pupils. This can only be done if teachers are given time and encouragement to discuss with their pupils the powerful agencies, Press, television, radio and film, which subtly shape their outlook and their lives. In the important publication *Liberal Education in a Technical Age* produced some years ago by a committee for the National Institute of Adult Education the following words appear:

> We regard a liberal education as one which includes a training in the use of language, in the handling of ideas, in recognising relationships, and in establishing values as touchstones by which questions of taste and morals are to be tested.

If this view is accepted, then the part played by the teacher in the secondary school in stimulating discussion and critical judgement becomes central in the whole educational process. It is to be noted that this type of education, once again, does not lend itself to any form of external examination. Nor can it be given at great speed or at any given speed; it may often require what Maritain has called 'an oriental sense of time'.

And it will demand, continually, the highest personal qualities of the teacher; worthiness of example, integrity of thought, humility in argument, clarity in expression, kindliness of heart and genuine sympathy with the youngster who comes from a home where most of the values for which the teacher stands are negatived. It is in such work as this, rather than in cramming facts and in developing skills which will satisfy the examiner, that the secondary teacher of today truly practises his art and fulfils his vocation.

The effect of the mass media on values of young people was forcefully raised in a letter given pride of place in *The Times* of May 9th, 1962. It was written by Mr. K. G. Collier, the Principal of the College of the Venerable Bede in the University of Durham. Here is an extract from it:

> It is of the greatest importance that teachers should more widely accept the responsibility of developing the discrimination of young viewers.
>
> The Society for Education in Film and Television has been pioneering this work for years; in October, 1960, the National Union of Teachers organised a large conference in London on the subject; and the British Film Institute has been giving all possible aid; yet the proportion of teachers who discuss television programmes with their pupils is, according to Dr. Himmelweit, still no more than 6 per cent. It is high time that the Ministry of Education gave a vigorous lead.

I agree with Mr. Collier that television programmes should be regularly discussed in schools, but I would like to see this firmly established by the teachers themselves, without any Ministry lead.

Preparing young people for a co-operating world

There is, too, another great change which is required of secondary education by humanity's plight today, one which is closely related to the development of critical thought, namely the creation of attitudes of tolerance, associated with the desire to understand and co-operate, even with groups living

under entirely different political systems. It we look closely
at secondary education in the major countries of the world,
including, however anachronistically, our own in this group,
we shall find almost no evidence of any general recognition
of such purposes as a legitimate part of secondary education.
In spite of the lip service to such ideals by official spokesmen at
international educational conferences where governments are
represented, there is no sincere attempt to follow words by
actions in this field. We have, in G. K. Chesterton's biting
words, only 'the empty speeches that comfort cruel men'
and each educational system goes on plugging its own political
and economic creed with no objective attempt to understand
or to interpret the other or to prepare for possible co-operation.
Even for richer co-operation among nations of the western
bloc it would appear that education has no part to play;
exchange of teachers between the United Kingdom and the
United States remains almost at the same figure as when the
scheme was started thirty years ago and outside the English-
speaking countries exchanges take place only as a means of
improving the speaking of the foreign languages studied in
school. We do not exchange physical education teachers with
Sweden, or music teachers with Italy or handicraft teachers with
Holland, even though in such subjects the language obstacle
is almost negligible.

But what we really need, when we have sufficiently built up
the study of Russian and Chinese[4] in our secondary schools,
is a wide-scale interchange of teachers with the U.S.S.R. and
China: at the human level at which all teaching takes place
understanding and co-operation are easy to achieve.

Yet, within the secondary school curriculum itself there is not
at present, in any country which I have visited, provision for
the kind of study which could prepare the way for a co-
operating world.

In the U.S.A. that combination of history and geography
known as social studies offers possibilities for promoting
world understanding. But in a country conditioned to a state
of almost religious faith in private enterprise objective study

of any country which has some 'socialized' institutions, not least 'socialized medicine', is very difficult.

In the United Kingdom geography offers the greatest hope, but some examination syllabuses at 'O' level need a slight adjustment or tilt so that the objective overall view may be taken. The following phrasing, from the section (c) Human Geography, of the Oxford and Cambridge Schools Board syllabus, 1960, provides splendid possibilities:

> Distribution of population and modes of living in relation to natural vegetation and cultivated crops, mineral wealth, and industrial development; lives of communities and transport, and the bearing of these on world problems.

One would have considered geography an essential study for any adolescent today; yet if one examines the G.C.E. statistics for England and Wales one finds that only about half of 'O' level candidates are entered in this subject. In most schools it is regarded as an *optional* subject to be dropped in favour of some other such as history or a second language, or science. One of the factors in reducing the number of subjects in which candidates have entered is, of course, the high pass mark of about 50 per cent introduced by the Secondary Schools Examination Council when they scrapped the School Certificate after the war, see p. 85.

Yet even outside the curriculum, schools prepare their pupils for international understanding only so far as the individual concern and sacrifice of free time by a few teachers makes this possible through the formation of an International Society or a branch of the Council for Education in World Citizenship. In this organization the United Kingdom has something of which the teaching profession, who made it, can be proud; all the more so because, so far as I am aware, no similar organization exists in any other country of the world. It exists as a service agency to provide schools that ask for it with help regarding facts concerning all aspects of international co-operation. It also arranges the great Christmas Vacation Conferences for Sixth Form pupils at Westminster Hall which are now famous and which provide one of the most remarkable audiences of keen young minds assembled anywhere in the world. The Board of Education, of pre-war years, was bold enough to give to this body, otherwise existing mainly on the subscriptions paid by pupils of the schools, a small subsidy which has now, under the Ministry of Education, fallen in the current year to £500.

When one compares this sum with the hundreds of millions of pounds spent on 'defence' one perceives the bitter truth of the remark made by Mr. J. B. Priestley at the founding of Unesco; 'Nations are always willing to spend money on their fears, but seldom on their hopes.'

In France there is an organization with branches in schools and universities which has somewhat the same objective, but ties itself closely with Unesco and is known as 'Friends of Unesco'. But most countries, in this field of promoting international understanding, have organized nothing at all for their schools.[5]

CHAPTER NINE

Technical Education for Adolescents and Day Release

TECHNICAL education, like other aspects of education in Great Britain, suffers a great deal from its long history. If it were possible now to start *ab initio*, and to build a system related to present and future needs, such a system would probably look very different indeed from what holds now. In particular, it would be possible to avoid the seeming chaos of today's institutions and to arrive at some common basis for entry into the lower grades of skilled work, those designated at present by the name 'craftsman'.

Apprenticeship in England and Wales

Today, as for hundreds of years, craftsmen are still trained by becoming apprenticed to an employer. This, on the face of it, especially where this means a personal interest of the employer, or of one of his personnel managers, in the individual apprentice, is a very fine thing. Unfortunately, in the face of industrial competition from abroad this system shows its leaks. Firstly, there is no form of examination, practical or theoretical, which the apprentice is required to take at the end of his period of indentures. He will have become a craftsman merely by the passage of time. Of course, in fairly large well-organized concerns it is possible to arrange for the apprentice to have a broad and thorough training, associated with theoretical studies provided by day-release attendance at a Technical College, and the training so provided by many firms is of a very high order. Yet, in spite of local apprentice committees set up jointly by employers and by Trade Unions in

9

many areas it has proved impossible to be certain that even a passable standard of training is given to all apprentices. This is understandable because, to take a typical example, a small firm of builders, pressed with urgent repair work due to bad weather, may not only have for some weeks to change all their working plans for their apprentice or apprentices, but also to hold them back from their weekly attendance at the Technical College and this gap, of course, makes subsequent understanding of their theoretical work difficult.

Secondly, there are maximum age limits[1] imposed by Trade Unions, for the recruitment of apprentices. These are aimed at ensuring that journeyman status (and consequent rate of pay) are achieved by the age of 21 years. Since the period of apprenticeship is usually five years this means that indentures must be signed before the youngster is 16 years of age. Although various loopholes have been made whereby an additional year of schooling after the age of 15 can be recognized in certain cases as equivalent to a year of apprenticeship, the general effect of the Trade Union regulation, though not intentional, is to deter some brighter boys from becoming craftsmen and to encourage thousands to leave school at the earliest moment. It must also be pointed out that in Sweden, Germany and France, the training of a craftsman, to a comparable level, is achieved in a number of trades in three years of apprenticeship plus *compulsory* part-time schooling from which the employer may not hold back his pupil, save in the direst need such as flood or tempest. Four years is required in some trades in Sweden and Germany, but rarely indeed are five years necessary.

As a result of the activities of various groups, including notably B.A.C.I.E.[2] the facts concerning apprenticeship in countries of Western Europe have been successfully brought to the attention of some Trade Unions, to many employers and more widely among educationists.[3] As a result a first move towards compressing but not diluting the apprentice training in the building industry was made in 1962 by reducing the period of indentures to four years. Other industries may be expected to follow suit. There is also the hope that the Training Act of 1963 will enable us to make up rapidly some of the leeway between Western Europe and ourselves in the field of industrial education.

Practical tests for journeymen

Yet the most serious shortcoming in the field of technical education at the lower levels is that for many industries there is no recognized basic qualification at the craftsman level, so there is nothing at which the young worker, boy or girl, can aim. Equally, of course, there is, in such cases, no standard of competence upon which the employer can rely.

In Sweden, Germany and France, a practical test of competence is an essential part of gaining journeyman qualification, and this qualification is available for almost every type of skilled industrial and commercial work, ranging from wine-making at one end through all the normal industrial and commercial skills to selling tourism at the other. Failure in the practical test can, of course, be redeemed in a subsequent attempt so the examiners, who include in all these countries representatives of the three interests concerned (employers, Trade Unions and technical teachers), have no compunction in failing students who cannot maintain the standard of the trade. In all these countries there is, consequently, real pride in holding journeyman qualification; the young worker has much more than mere concern to obtain journeyman's rate of pay. Of course, it is also true that in England ambitious and keen young workers set out to gain the qualifications of the City and Guilds of London Institute. But two points must be made against valuing this situation too highly. Firstly, there is no *obligation* upon an apprentice to pass any examination, and secondly, the theoretical part of the City and Guilds examinations often bulks so large in proportion to the practical test that the long-standing high rate of drop-out and failure is more due to inability to grapple with the written part of the examination than to inability to show the necessary practical skill. This matter is well known but there has been little success in trying to improve the situation. The Ministry of Education in its Annual Report 1956 (in the section dealing with Technical Education) § 23 stated:

One noticeable feature of these figures is the high percentage of failures which they disclose. Some students succeed at the second or third attempt, but too many fail to pass. It is impossible to determine precisely how far these failures are due to lack of facilities in technical colleges, lack of time for adequate study, or lack of ability on the part of the candidates themselves. Clearly, however, there is much room for improvement and it is hoped that the steps which have been and are being taken to improve and expand college facilities, by providing more and better buildings and equipment will gradually alter the picture. In particular, the establishment of more branch and local colleges to relieve regional colleges of their lower level work will enable students to have more facilities nearer to their homes and to spend less time in travelling. Lack of time results also from the intensive character of some of the courses and from the fact that so many of the students attend only in the evenings. What is needed here is a more general change-over from attendance at evening classes to attendance at part-time day courses, with perhaps a broadening and lengthening of the courses themselves. Lack of ability can only be met by restricting the admission of students to those courses in which they are likely to succeed. Ways of surmounting these difficulties were under consideration during the year.

The failure rate is of such significance to the lives of the young workers that the Church of England Board of Education in April 1960, expressing the view that the time had come to rethink the content of education in Technical Colleges, added:

Technical Colleges have grown up mainly in response to the needs of industry, developing a proliferation of specialised courses leading to examinations which, as the high failure rate shows, are often unsuited to the students accepted for them.

Since the failures are mainly in the written part of the

examination, and not in the practical work, suggestions have been coming forward that tests based mainly on practical work, as in France and Germany, should be developed.

In *The Times* of August 17th, 1962, the Labour Correspondent of that newspaper, writing of a report just issued by the Industrial Training Council, complains that this report contains no reference to independent testing of young men who have gone through industrial apprenticeships, saying that such testing is the rule in other industrial countries like West Germany, France and Sweden.

Apprenticeship in France

In France a large proportion of 'journeymen', whether fitters or typists, have gained their 'Certificate of Professional Aptitude' without having been indentured to an employer. Instead they will have gained their qualification by a three-year full-time course involving 40 hours per week of theoretical and practical studies for something like the normal school terms, usually obtaining temporary employment in their trade during part of their summer vacation. This type of course, which was only started on a large scale after the Liberation, and for which all the teachers, both technical and general, were gradually given special training, has proved to be so immensely successful that, under the Educational Reform Act passed by de Gaulle's Government on January 7th, 1959, the Apprenticeship Centres where such training was given were dignified with the new name of *Collèges d'Enseignement Technique*. For some years now more than 300,000 young men and women have been completing, by the age of 18, their three-year courses of industrial and commercial training. When, in 1967, no French adolescent abandons full-time education of some form before the age of 16+ (*i.e.*, the end of the school year in which he reaches the age of 16) all the apprentices who at present obtain their qualifications by indentured arrangements together with the theoretical studies made obligatory under the Loi Astier of 1919, will enter *Collèges d'Enseignement Technique*. Unfortunately, no such prospect exists for apprentices in England in 1967, or even subsequently.

It is true that at one stage, when the British government was endeavouring to persuade industry to act on the findings of the Carr Report and to increase the places for apprentices and to increase the proportion of young workers given day release, Sir David Eccles in the House of Commons threatened that the government might introduce the French system:

> Today, with nearly 500,000 students on day release, I am sorry to see that the annual rate of increase has slowed right down. Therefore the Government must take some important decisions about the possible lines of advance.
>
> Sooner or later the Government will have to decide whether to continue to base their arrangements mainly on the present system, which puts on industry the primary responsibility for training their young workers, or whether to make a major change to something like the French system, under which about one-third of their young people get their further education and initial industrial training before going into employment.[4]

But everyone knew, of course, that this was the merest bluff and that the situation both in technical colleges and in teacher training was such that, even if the unimaginable situation were to arise in which the government were willing to contemplate large-scale expenditure, no project could be envisaged of teachers being available either for the technical or general education of the apprentice courses.

Day-release of young workers in England and Wales

It is to be hoped that by the time these words are in print, either as a result of the recommendations of the Henniker–Heaton Committee, or in some other way, the Minister of Education may have succeeded in his plans to increase considerably the attendance of young workers at day-release classes.

Meanwhile it should be noted that the latest figures at present available regarding the attendance of young workers at day-release classes are:

Boys and girls under 18 years of age attending day release

during the school year 1961–62 . . . 262,350, which represents 12 per cent of the age group. Breakdown figures for the separate years of age are given below:

Age on 1st Aug. 1960	Boys on day release	Girls on day release
15	51,712	15,171
16	82,058	21,939
17	74,408	17,062
18	54,793	5,803
19	40,915	2,745
20	30,953	1,640

These figures represent approximately one boy in three in employment under 18 years of age and less than one girl in ten.[5] In Germany the figure has been 100 per cent for both boys and girls for nearly forty years.

So no consideration of day release is adequate that does not draw attention to the *Berufsschulen* of Germany and to the fact that in these schools the Germans brought to fruition, in 1919 and 1920, throughout Germany, the idea which had been incorporated in the 1918 'Fisher' Education Act of the United Kingdom.

In this Act it had been laid down that from an 'appointed day' which would be settled by the Board of Education with each separate L.E.A.,[6] taking into account its preparedness, there should be established Day Continuation Schools. These would be attended one day per week up to the age of 16 by boys and girls who were at work. The annual total of hours was to be 320, but in the first seven years of implementation the L.E.A. might reduce this to 280 hours. Thereafter the top age of compulsory attendance was to be raised from 16 to 18. Unfortunately, reactionary forces, stimulated and supported by an absurd 'anti-waste' campaign organized by a powerful Press group, caused these clauses of the Act to be nullified. Even the Day Continuation Schools already established in London and West Ham, some of them showing remarkable developments within a few months, had to be closed.

Meanwhile, in 1919, the French government passed the

Loi Astier, commonly known in that country as 'The Charter of Technical Education', to the provisions of which reference has already been made. To provide funds for this technical education a *Taxe d'Apprentissage* was applied to all employers of young workers.

We have, in preceding pages, touched upon one aspect of the post-Liberation expansion of technical education in France. Whether or not this has paid off can best be judged by the post-1944 development of the French economy. Here, for instance, is a quotation from *The Times* of July 6th, 1962—*i.e.*, during a year when British productivity was falling in many sectors of industry and failing to rise in most others:

> The French economy is continuing to expand, according to Minister of Finance, Giscard d'Estaing. The Minister told the National Assembly that during May the industrial production index rose to 199 against 184 in May 1961, twice as high as in 1952.

Berufsschulen in Germany

The year 1919 was also the one in which the Germans introduced their law making attendance one day per week at *Berufsschulen* compulsory for all young workers under 18 years of age. The courses, in every case, were built round the type of work for which the young person had entered, on the principles magnificently worked out by Kerschensteiner, Director of Education at Munich, in experimental day-release schools prior to the First World War. Whilst the conclusion of most courses is marked by the apprenticeship examination, since in Germany many more types of work are organized under apprentice indentures than in England and there is a recognized standard of achievement for qualification at journeyman level, there is no neglect of the semi-skilled and unskilled young workers. Instead, considerable pedagogical ingenuity has been displayed in constructing courses which involve skills and knowledge relevant to the job. Young postmen, railway porters, dockers,[7] girl machinists in factories for garments or plastic toys, and so on and so forth, all these young workers have special courses built around their daily job as the centre of interest, often with special textbooks. They all also have civic studies, organized visits and, frequently, class holidays together. Even for the educationally subnormal there are special activities in the *Berufsschulen*.

The most important effect of these schools, in my opinion, is the effect that they have had upon the morale of the young worker. Jenny Lind sang, 'Be it ever so humble, there's no place like home'. The signature tune of many *Berufsschulen* might be 'Be it ever so humble, there's no work like mine'. They give dignity to labour and to the labourer by investing even the lowliest forms of work with a certain measure of expertise which can be talked about and learned. For all attending the *Berufsschulen* for semi-skilled and unskilled workers there are, both for boys and for girls, courses of instruction in physical skills required in running a home. When one considers that *every* German boy and girl young worker under 18 years of age has had the advantage of such courses of training since 1920, is it fanciful to find a connection between these courses and the astounding recovery of West German industry after all the devastation of the war? Of course, other influences, not least American money, have played their part, but is it ridiculous to suppose that the relative absence of strikes and the almost complete, if not complete, absence of wild cat strikes is connected with the combination of pride in one's job and some knowledge of the mechanisms that ensure the smooth functioning of civic life?

There is one further thing to be learned from the outstanding successes of Sweden, Germany and France in the field of technical education at craftsman level and lower, namely that the vocational approach to education clearly meets the psychological needs of a considerable proportion of adolescents. In the Swedish Comprehensive Middle Schools although everyone stays within the educative framework till the end of the school year in which he reaches the age of 16, something like half of the pupils in their last year of 'schooling' are spending half of their time in the first stages of their chosen work, the half in school being appropriately geared. In the previous year they will have had three or four work experiences of not less than a week in a chosen variety of forms of work, under conditions which enable them, the employer and the guidance officer to form a pretty accurate opinion of the degree of success they will meet in the given job. Thus even the penultimate year of schooling is frankly concerned with vocational interests and not just with education for education's sake, which is the formula of far too many people in this country.

For example, pupils who have chosen work in fields where specialized technical training is needed, particularly in which special equipment or machinery is required, will attend appropriate courses half-time at what we would call the local Technical College. Their school will provide continuing general education including language studies and science and mathematics as may be desirable and, of course, physical education and cultural activities.

A contrasting example is that of girls who wish to become saleswomen in shops; they will work at a shop half the week and have general studies, including the elements of commerce and kindred subjects, in the school. Sometimes the half-time is arranged by alternating weeks at work and at school, according to the nature of the work and the most efficient way of organizing the combination of work and study.

In the case of agriculture long period alternation is necessary for town boys. Thus boys from the city of Gothenburg who wish to have an agricultural career spend weeks of spring and early autumn at Jordhammars residential School of Agriculture and Agricultural Machinery some 25 miles away and study science and general subjects when back at school.

There is every indication in Sweden that this arrangement for the boys and girls who do not wish to continue full-time school education after the age of 15+ is working well. With the further evidence of the success of the non-academic Apprenticeship Centres (now *Collèges d'Enseignement Technique*) in France, of the *Berufsschulen* in Germany and, if we would accept it as evidence, of the Vocational Schools of the U.S.S.R. and East Germany, we should be well advised to make compulsory day-release our first priority for the education of those under 18.

There is, however, another point of view which is sometimes put forward. It was eloquently expressed by Mr. W. S. Howard, Deputy Chairman of the Warwickshire Education Committee, in his presidential address in June 1962 to the Association of Education Committees. Having suggested that perhaps the time had come for a new Education Act, he went on to say:

> It may be . . . that we should write into a new Education Act, not the setting up of county colleges for part-time day release, but the future raising of the school leaving age to 18. The growth of automation should quite soon make it practicable.
>
> Education for all to the age of 18 would pre-suppose that there were no financial road blocks for those who wanted to continue their education after that age.[8]

I disagree profoundly with this view. I am concerned not with far-fetched policies which cannot be implemented within twenty years, but with doing something *now* which may improve the educational opportunities for those children already born and shortly to seek secondary and higher education. Moreover, I am strongly of the opinion that it is far more important first to extend the provision of voluntary day-release and secondly to introduce compulsory day-release than to raise the school leaving age even to 16. The reasons for this view can be summarized as follows:

(1) The earlier maturity of adolescents increases rather than diminishes their desire for independence—*i.e.*, for starting on their own industrial, commercial or professional path.

(2) While continuation of full-time academic secondary schooling *is* the only path for a professional career and many types of commercial career and some types of industrial career, yet for a great many types of work, both industrial and commercial, it is irrelevant.

(3) Secondary education, except that in some secondary technical schools, is so steeped in the academic tradition

that there can be no real hope of secondary schools as a whole adapting themselves within the next decade to meeting the needs of those boys and girls who would resent *being compelled* to stay on at school beyond the age of 15. Those who voluntarily stay on constitute a different kettle of fish. For evidence of this we have the figures provided by Professor D. V. Glass which have been given and discussed in a previous chapter.

(4) Even if adolescents are all compelled to stay at school till the age of 16, this addition of one year's reluctant schooling to, say, 50 per cent of the age group constitutes a very small theoretical gain for a very large operation and considerable expenditure. What we should be aiming at is *not* an extra year of schooling for half an age group, but a helpful surveillance of all young workers up to the age of 18, the continuance of the habits of learning established while at school, and the joyful recognition that life and life-long learning are the Siamese twins of the twenty-first century. And it is for that century, we hope, that we are educating most of the boys and girls who are at school now.

(5) The industrial and economic situation of the United Kingdom at present is such that if she is to play a worthy part, whether in relation to the Common Market or to the Commonwealth, every effort should be made to increase productivity and to improve industrial relations. There is no hope of any increased productivity resulting from keeping at secondary school for an extra year boys and girls who do not wish to stay. But there *is* hope that day-release, with its mixture of vocational, general and civic education, as defined in Section 43 of the Education Act of 1944, *would*, within a year or two, have a positive effect both upon productivity and upon industrial relations. Moreover, this section of the Act was in 1944 given a clear priority and represented a second attempt within thirty years to do something which other nations have already done and shown to be worth while. If the

government were to decide *now* that this part of the Act would be enforced in 1967, though we should still be behind the French, at that time, we should have just succeeded in implementing an idea within half a century of having it put upon the Statute Book.

As for technical education at all levels above that of the craftsman, though there is much to be desired in some sections, it is not only in far better shape as a whole, but is steadily developing on a broad front. The creation of the Colleges of Advanced Technology was achieved in the nick of time and their subsequent upward pull upon Technical Colleges as a whole has been stupendous and is still continuing.

It would be appropriate to end this chapter by quoting the first paragraph of the important Section 43 of the Education Act 1944:

43 (1) On and after such date as His Majesty may by Order in Council determine, not later than three years after the date of the commencement of this Part of this Act (The Statutory System of Education) it shall be the duty of every local education authority to establish and maintain county colleges, that is to say, centres approved by the Minister for providing for young persons who are not in full-time attendance at any school or other educational institution such further education, including physical, practical and vocational training, as will enable them to develop their various aptitudes and capacities and will prepare them for the responsibilities of citizenship.

CHAPTER TEN

Higher and Further Education

THE absurd order of the two adjectives in the title of this chapter is deliberate. Of course, in accepted practice Further Education refers to part-time day release, evening classes, full-time classes at Technical Colleges and Colleges of Art and so on. Higher Education, in the minds of most people, means the Universities and the Colleges of Advanced Technology; so the Teacher Training Colleges seem to float somewhere in between, like the angels between God and man.

But it is the problem of university admissions which is going to hit us sooner and harder than any problem of Further Education, although the two branches cannot be discussed apart any longer.

Of course, everyone is keenly—or anxiously—awaiting the Report of the Robbins Committee. Its terms of reference are:

> To review the pattern of full-time higher education in Great Britain and in the light of national needs and resources to advise Her Majesty's Government on what principles its long-term development should be based. In particular, to advise, in the light of these principles, whether there should be any changes in that pattern, whether any new types of institution are desirable and whether any modification should be made in the present arrangements for planning and co-ordinating the development of the various types of institution.

We know that the Committee have made extensive trips abroad; and inspired sources have told us that the mass of sociological data which the Committee has caused to be prepared for it is likely to be a source of delight to sociologists for several years. These are splendid portents and we are justified in expecting the far-sighted Report that this country badly needs. Then the vital question arises—what will the Government *do* about it? The danger of a bold, imaginative report is simply that Whitehall, and particularly the Treasury, will be aghast at it.

The situation was brilliantly summed up in an article entitled 'Razor's Edge' in *The Times* monthly publication *Techology* in September 1962. Here is an extract:

> Indeed it is true that nobody knows what the Robbins Committee will say—if the future of British higher education depended on that verdict it would not be poised on a razor's edge; it would be on a needle's point, free to fall in every direction. A Committee can say anything, but reality is not so versatile; and in the last resort it is the people who actually have to implement executive decisions, who determine what they are to be. Some time ago in these columns was made a distinction between two sorts of committee reporting on matter of public policy. One sort consists of the eminent, the high principled and the public spirited and produces a report that is far-seeing and right. That kind of report is shelved. The other sort consists of men who adequately represent the sectional interests involved, and produces a report which is cautious enough to protect those interests. That kind of report is usually adopted and its provisions are made to work at one of the characteristic English speeds of slow, dead slow, or stop.

If this analysis be correct, then there is no hope of any changes of significance that might take place in less than ten years.

So the following views represent not a far-seeing plan, not any attempt to tidy up chaos, but suggestions of things which might be done quickly, if there were a feeling of urgency, to meet the needs of the boys and girls of the birth-rate bulge when they demand Higher Education in 1965.

The unhealthy competition for university entrance and the resulting oedematous Sixth Form

For many years now, as a result of the extended public financial aid to university students, there have been far more applicants than places. As a result the standard for admission has been raised. This, of course, does not mean that the standard *of* admission has been raised. All it means is that in those universities where before the war admission used to be dependent upon having passed certain examinations in certain subjects at certain levels, admission is now based upon higher levels of examination achievement, even if the number of subjects is smaller, as it is in almost all cases.

Before the Second World War boys and girls, as a rule, spent only two years in the Sixth Form entering, on one occasion only, for the Higher School Certificate. On the result of this examination most boys and girls who had sought it gained admission to Redbrick universities and many gained scholarships. Only for the competition for Open Scholarships at Oxbridge, as a rule, did boys and girls spend a third year in the Sixth. Today, as a result of the fierce battle for all university places, able boys and girls are hurried through the main secondary school course, often to the detriment of their ability at games, or with a musical instrument, or to their interests in scouting and so. They can then spend three years in the Sixth Form (and occasionally even more) and so take the G.C.E. 'A' level examinations twice.

Many, perhaps most, of those who are candidates for universities pass the examination in their chosen subjects on the first occasion, but fail to get a mark high enough, in this intense competition, to defeat those who are taking the examination for a second, or even third, time. So they spend a further year in the Sixth Form, take the examination again and, in most cases, then land themselves places in a university. Meanwhile the Sixth Form suffers from oedema.

So we should consider the whole situation. Firstly, we note that the boy or girl who is ultimately accepted is, in most cases, a person who, but for the excessive competition, might well have been admitted a year earlier. The native intelligence of the candidate, which is the chief thing that matters to a university, will have been in no way improved by a year of further cramming for an examination.

Secondly, in many cases no important new work has been

learned by the candidate during the extra year. If it has, the gain is illusory, for such work is usually dealt with again during the first year at the university. Indeed, university lecturers, especially in science, often complain that work has been tackled at school which cannot be dealt with adequately there and that the students are bored when it is repeated, even if adequately, at the university. The lecturers add that a broader, stronger foundation would have been much more helpful.

Thirdly, when it comes to that refinement of examination answers which is essential for the gaining of high marks, then the quality of the *teaching* often matters more than the quality of the student. Anyone who has had experience of marking sets of G.C.E. papers knows that, in effect, the examination is more a test of the quality of the teaching than of the ability of the candidate. Indeed, in examinations of this kind it can hardly be otherwise.

We can, then, draw the paradoxical conclusion that the fiercer the competition for places in the Redbrick universities, the less satisfactory the body of students that they admit. This is emphasized by the situation in the science subjects. There is a grave shortage of good teachers of science, particularly in the Grammar Schools for girls, in some of which the science staff are not only inadequate in number, but inexperienced and rather mediocre teachers. So the university selection is primarily, though unintentionally, a matter of selecting schools from which it will accept students rather than of selecting the best students from all the schools.

In a recent article[1] Professor R. A. C. Oliver of the University of Manchester has drawn attention to a very different method of selection of university students which has been used with considerable success for a long time by a number of leading universities in the U.S.A. Certainly something is needed to reduce the extent to which selection for university education is, to such an unduly high degree as at present, selection of the candidates who have been the best taught.

Before any attempt is made to put forward a suggestion we

10

ought to note the effects upon Grammar Schools in general and upon the public purse of the widespread development of a separate third year Sixth Form—sometimes called the Seventh Form. Because so much potential glory to the school is at stake, heads of schools and governing bodies spare no efforts, within the financial limits which control them, to appoint for work with this group of pupils the ablest teachers they can find. These teachers, therefore, after the Head and the Deputy Head are, very often, the highest paid members of the staff of day schools. Certainly they are *among* the highest paid members of the staff and certainly the groups of students whom they teach are likely to be the smallest groups taught in the school and often uneconomically small. The cost of teaching a pupil in the third year Sixth is therefore likely to be out of all proportion to the cost of teaching a pupil in the main body of the school and considerably higher, if all staff are taken into account, than the cost of teaching the first and second year Sixth Form pupil. To what end? To make him more intelligent, creative, self-reliant? No; for no teacher, however able, can improve a student's inherited packet of genes nor, by helping the student more, teach creativity, nor promote self-reliance by cramming him. The only effect that the teacher has is to enable *this* student to gain a place in a university instead of another who is rejected through being taught less well and must now either seek to enter a College of Advanced Technology, a Teacher Training College, pay for a place at an American or Commonwealth University or abandon his desire for Higher Education. The situation is manifestly absurd.

Emergency expansion of Higher Education

It is one thing to complain about what is wrong; it is, of course, another thing to find a way of putting the matter right, especially when the wrong is not the result of any malevolence but has developed as an honest attempt to do what is right in circumstances brought about by a policy inspired by the highest motives—namely to give financial support from public funds to university students on such a basis that no worthy student should be excluded as a result of having parents in a low income bracket.

There is only one way to solve this problem, namely to make considerable increases, by emergency measures, in the number of places available in the field of Higher Education.

At the same time it is important that the universities shall not suffer either from being grossly overcrowded or from having their standards lowered, or from both.

In any case, there is no possibility of the universities being able to take, in the next few years, the numbers they would have been prepared to take.[2] This is because of the persistent postponements and economies by two successive Chancellors of the Exchequer on the announced plans of university expansion. Every time these economies were made, public outcry was avoided by the disingenuous use of the word 'phasing' Now we have thousands of qualified young men and women for whom there are no places in universities, as well as more than 2,000 suitable applicants in 1962 for Teacher Training Colleges for whom there were no vacancies.

A university for rejects

John Margeson, an admissions tutor and lecturer in English at the University of Hull, who has also taught at Cambridge and at several Canadian universities, in a broadcast in November 1962 stated:

> I have been concerned with university admissions for several years, both in this country and abroad, and I have been growing increasingly worried about the young people we turn away from our universities and the talent that is going to waste. It is difficult to find out exactly how many qualified applicants the universities reject every year. It may already be as high as 10,000, and the number is growing.

Mr. Margeson went on to suggest, as a means of quickly salvaging some of these students, 'A University for Rejects', using emergency housing and teaching arrangements:

To meet an urgent need we might have to take over assembly halls, barns and warehouses. The students will have to rough it. I would like to see them establish co-operative houses of their own and run their own restaurants. They could adapt Nissen huts from nearby airfields. Under these conditions they might learn to live together as true communities. Few of the great halls of residence we have put up in recent years have developed into communities of any kind. This shoe-string budget might force us back to a more lively concept of a university. We have come to regard universities as expensive institutions, demanding from the start a huge capital outlay on laboratories, lecture rooms and libraries. . . .

What about the curriculum? I will just say that I would favour a four-year course for the honours degree, with the additional year to counteract the dangers of too much specialisation. But on one point I am firm: the basic programme of studies should not be imposed from above as a rigid and permanent system. I feel strongly that the experience of the whole teaching staff should be used in working out a flexible curriculum that is capable of change and development. To my mind, there is no doubt at all that a university for rejects is urgently needed. It is an eminently practical proposal and one that is unique in appealing equally to the conservative and the radical, to the hard-headed and the visionary. In fact there seems to be no good reason why work should not begin on the project immediately.[3]

Whilst there is much to be said for this suggestion—and there are probably sufficient disused airfields to enable several universities for rejects to be started—it does not seem that these would introduce into our system of Higher Education any new elements capable of providing for the continuous expansion of demand for education at this level. Instead we should organize Community Colleges somewhat along the lines of those that have been running successfully for many years in the United States. They would probably emerge so different from the American ones that we should be adopting only the name— a very good one under which to extend Higher Education.

The case for Community Colleges

These institutions should offer first year, and probably even second year, university work to day students of university calibre who have not, however, succeeded in winning places at universities, preferably *on their first attempt* at 'A' level.

Instead of staying on at school, repeating work which they have already done, they would continue to advance their studies along university lines for a further year, while still living at home. At the end of this year several possibilities should be open to them.

Firstly, there should be the opportunity to continue studies at the Community Colleges along 'applied' lines, instead of the 'pure' lines of most university studies. These might prepare them for social work of all kinds (including new developments), for local government, commerce and so on, leading to rather higher qualifications than are available at the majority of 'Local' Technical Colleges. Indeed, the qualifications would mostly tend to be of Pass Degree standard at the end of a further two years of study. Three or four subjects might well be required for the qualification and permit new combinations of studies likely to be of particular relevance to the improvement of our ways of life, moral, intellectual and physical. Incidentally, there is much to be done with regard to the welfare of the coloured members of our population and social workers of many kinds are likely to be in increasing demand in the years ahead.

Language studies, too, could be highly developed, with a wide range of possibilities, in Community Colleges. But the nature of the provision of second and third year courses in Community Colleges would vary from one locality to another.

For, at the end of the first year, many of the students on the Science side would wish to apply for entry to Colleges of Advanced Technology, to National Colleges of technology of various kinds, to Regional Technical Colleges or to Area Technical Colleges, assuming that their own 'Local' Technical College does not offer courses leading to External Degrees of London University or to other qualifications of a comparable standard. Many Arts students, too, now a year older and so more suited for the rough-and-tumble of life in lodgings, would be prepared to leave home and live in a city where a

Polytechnic or comparable institution is offering part-time courses leading to an External Degree. It is even possible that other students, especially as Community Colleges established themselves, might be admitted in the second year of universities, to fill places of those who had fallen by the way.

The important thing is that Community Colleges could be widespread and immediate, and would make use of and integrate with all local educational services, especially of course all forms of Further Education, including Technical Colleges, of whatever level, within reach. The object of Community Colleges would not be to compete with any existing educational provision, but to supplement it with new opportunities, particularly in new fields of study.

Premises for Community Colleges and their staffing

For most 'Arts' subjects the only physical provision which is absolutely essential is a room where the students can sit and a blackboard on which the lecturer can chalk. Emergency conditions need emergency measures and because many school and university classrooms are empty in the evenings there is no reason why Community College students should not have their lectures in evenings and do their private study at home by day. Indeed, it might well result in a higher standard of work since only the very best lectures make as much demand upon the powers of the intellect as a good text-book or as writing an essay for a tutor.

So a Community College need not, in the first emergency stage, have a building of its own. It must have an office and central planning organization, but for the first few years it need no more have its own ferro-concrete structure than an organization such as the College of the Teachers of the Deaf, which is a corporate body with an office and no teaching premises at all.

As for the social life which one has at a university, one can only repeat that emergency conditions need emergency measures and it is better for would-be students to miss the social side of university life than to miss Higher Education completely. In any case, where there is a will, and particularly where there is youth, community life can be established under umpromising conditions.

As for the lecturers, there are several sources of emergency supply—retired university lecturers, most of whom are still at a remarkable pitch of efficiency at the age of 65, teachers who would be freed from the closed down Seventh Forms and university lecturers working overtime. Such is the extent of underpayment of university lecturers that many of them, for the support of their family, are prepared to delay their researches a little when offered payment for an extra-mural course of lectures.

No one could say that the scheme sketched above is either attractive or tidy, but it is offered as being much better than the alternative of *nothing* in 1965 and 1966 for tens of thousands of would-be students. Moreover, many educational institutions which have subsequently developed magnificent buildings, whether they be Birbeck College or the Medical Research Council Cancer Laboratories, or the Institut Pasteur, began in hired rooms, ex-army huts and a cellar as these three, respectively, began their existence.

'Local' Technical Colleges as Community Colleges

In some towns where the Technical College has only 'Local' rank and where the premises are not fully used by day it may be possible to make the Technical College into a Community College by greatly widening its field of activity. This would involve Ministerial raising of the status of the College in the hierarchy of Technical Colleges, or at least raising the salary levels of the Principal and many of the lecturers.

Moreover the word 'Technical' would become more of a misnomer than it already is at present, for almost all of them teach many *pure* sciences and many, indeed, unblushingly teach 'arts' subjects without giving them the least suspicion of 'technical' bias. Provided the salary conditions were adequately improved there is no reason why university lecturers, active or retired, could not as well be recruited for occasional or part-time work by small 'Local' Technical Colleges as by the proposed Community Colleges or by the existing Colleges of Advanced Technology. Moreover, many small 'Local' Technical Colleges have already much experience of arranging courses of study in improvised lecture rooms and, clearly, improvisation must be the watchword of the next few years if a generation of young people is not to be deprived of proper opportunities of Higher Education. As for society's need of young people with this level of education in almost all walks of life, there is no need to convert anyone to this viewpoint— the advertisement pages of *The Times* and of the important Sunday newspapers have told this story for years. Moreover, such importance as Britain may have in the last decades of the twentieth century must inevitably reflect our level of intellectual achievement, since there is little else, fortunately perhaps, that it will be able to reflect.

Would a Community College adversely effect the Grammar Schools?

It is just possible that objection to Community Colleges might be raised by teachers at Grammar Schools, especially when the Seventh Form disappears. They might argue that the school would suffer from loss of very mature leaders.

On the contrary the development of Community Colleges, with the consequent extinction of the third year Sixth, would in fact minister to the general health of secondary education by enabling the opportunities of practising leadership to be offered to more and to younger pupils. Before the recent war, and even as late as a decade ago, it could still be argued that one of the reasons why a boy or girl should stay on at school, even if he or she did not wish to go on to the university, was that the Sixth Form gave its members the chance of playing leadership roles in games and in school societies of all kinds and even in school government. Today, with our top-heavy Grammar Schools, this is no longer true. A few pupils will hold such positions for two or even three years, but many Sixth Formers nowadays will leave school without having tasted any of the sweets and bitters of responsibility. Only recently a London Grammar School, advertising for a Physics Master, stated that there were 150 boys reading Physics in the Sixth Form. The size of the total Sixth Form in such a school is likely to be so great that the chances of leadership in any field of activity must be very small. If the young men and women who would otherwise stay on to be the Seventh Form or third year Sixth are removed to Community Colleges or Technical Colleges they can there play a part in building up the social and sports life of such institutions while leaving the opportunity for those a year younger than themselves to assume responsible positions in school life as used to be possible.

It may be that the Croydon suggestion of combining Sixth Forms will lead to experiments providing data for other changes in the way in which Grammar Schools are organized. But in my view it would be better to leave the first and second years of the Sixths alone, subject to the modifications already suggested, and to persuade schools and universities, by their joint action, to hand pupils over after that to Universities or to Community Colleges or to Technical Colleges of all kinds, or to Teacher Training Colleges.

CHAPTER ELEVEN

The Training of Teachers for Primary Schools

ALTHOUGH a great expansion of educational activities of all kinds is absolutely essential for the life of the nation, and although this will demand a great increase in the number of teachers, it will not be teachers for secondary schools who will be most in demand. For, as we have already pointed out, if films, radio, television, library and study halls are properly developed and used, and if part-time help is introduced into school libraries and study halls, and technicians are recruited for laboratories and for film projection and so on, then far more pupils can be truly educated with the existing number of teachers.

But for the primary school the problem is different; small classes there are absolutely essential and must be regarded as a priority in school reform. The immediate difficulty is two-fold. Firstly, there is a continuing high birth-rate. Secondly, the earlier age of marriage has produced special difficulties for the infant schools and the junior schools, for in these schools the teachers are, and ought to be, mainly women.

The term applied, very inappropriately, to the withdrawal (temporarily, if we arrange things properly) of women teachers on marriage or child-birth is 'wastage'! The following figures, taken from the Ministry of Education publication *The Demand and Supply of Teachers 1960–1980*, June 1962,[1] shows how the future situation is envisaged at present:

Wastage rates of non-graduate women teachers
(Years ending 31st March)

Age at beginning of year	1961/2	1964/5	1969/70
Under 24	10·7	11·7	12·5
24–28	18·3	20·3	21·9
29–38	10·3	11·8	13·1
39–48	3·0	3·5	4·0
49–58	3·0	3·2	3·4
59 and over	28·8	25·0	25·0

Figures are percentages of the teachers in each age group.

At present no young woman can become a qualified teacher by means of the Training College route before an effective age of 21 years. For she may not commence at a Training College until she is at least 18 years of age. From this table it can be calculated that nearly two-thirds of these women will have given less than seven years of service before leaving the profession and that about one in four will have given less than three years. Indeed, if hunches were as valuable as statistics (and they sometimes are) one would guess that the figure of 11·7 in the second column will be proved in due course to have been too low. For women graduate teachers the figures are little different.

In a subsequent publication of the Ministry of Education, *The Future Pattern of the Education and Training of Teachers*,[2] we read:

> If the 1960/1 rate of wastage were to get no worse, only about fifty out of every hundred young women entering service would still be teaching after five years. It seems prudent to expect that this rate of wastage will in fact increase. We are, therefore, assuming that it will worsen up to 1970, to the extent that of every hundred young women entering then and thereafter only about forty will remain in service after five years.

Clearly, then, the recruitment of young women for teaching in primary schools is a matter of very great significance and we ought to look at more aspects of the problem.

Making allowance for maturity

Until 1960 young men and women entering Teacher Training Colleges at the age of 18 years were able to complete their training in two years. At the end of this time they went out to teach, mostly in primary and infant schools, but there were no general comments regarding their being too young for the job. Indeed, I have never once heard such a remark.

From 1960 the course of training was, no doubt rightly, extended by a year to three years, but there has been no corresponding reduction in the age of entry by one year. But I am strongly of the opinion that many young men and women of 17 years of age are mature enough to enter Training College and that it would be a very good thing to encourage such young people to do so. Firstly, their further maturing would be speeded up much faster than if they are required to remain at school in the Sixth Form for a further year. And, secondly, and much more important, they would be rescued from the clutches of the pseudo-scholarship of 'A' level specialization and examination and given an opportunity to begin that intellectual and social broadening which must be a particular strength and asset to the teacher in primary schools.

We have already quoted from Mr. Percy Wilson, H.M. Senior Chief Inspector, but it is justifiable at this juncture to repeat and extend his condemnation of Sixth Form studies[3]:

> It is anti-cultural as well as uneducational. It dis-prepares, rather than prepares, the boys and girls for the real business of university study, and equally for the real business of technology, commerce and the learned professions.

These words must apply with even greater force with regard to future teachers in primary schools for Mr. Wilson continues:

> Much of our work a year or so below the Sixth Form is hurried and congested beyond all reason. Much of it is untouched by any mark of modern thought and discovery and most of it, in most schools (the great public schools not excepted), is semi-specialised to a degree which, at the age of fourteen or fifteen, makes no sense at all and is indefensible in any circumstances, or by any

plea other than the naked admission of competitive pressures transmitted downwards from the age of eighteen.

Clearly, what young men and women who are to enter Teacher Training Colleges need in the Sixth Form is not to follow their previous years of semi-specialization by two or three years of intense specialization, but to have a general course, aimed at widening horizons and fostering 'The Unity of Knowledge' which was the subject of Mr. Wilson's address. Such courses used to be common in Sixth Forms, especially in girls' Grammar Schools. What is needed in the primary school teacher is *not* the academic approach with deep knowledge in two restricted fields, but a broad field of interests, an up-to-date knowledge of what is going on in the nation and in the world, an awareness of what is going on in the way of utilization of leisure in the homes of typical working-class families, some experience of foreign travel and, if possible, some linguistic skill in the day-to-day use of a foreign language. Moreover, since every teacher of small children has, in one way or another, to answer questions with regard to natural life and to scientific developments, the teacher needs to have a broad but quite elementary knowledge of ornithology, astronomy, geology, plant and animal life, human biology, simple electricity, the very elements of heat, light and sound, and enough knowledge of modern scientific developments as to be able to profit from the majority of the popular science programmes put over on television. Of course, some of this preparation is given in many Training Colleges, but a good broad introduction to these subjects at school is essential as a base on which to build.

In view of the necessity for a primary school teacher to know quite a lot about the life of the community—to have sat in Magistrates' Courts, visited child clinics, hospitals, homes for aged people, fire stations, sewage works, water works, electricity generating stations, it is obvious that the best preparation, in the Sixth Forms, is a two year general course without examination. Such courses used to exist but are becoming less and less common.

The reason? The old Adam, and still more the old Eve, in

the Lecturers and in the Principals of most Training Colleges. The lack of post-war planning and the government's unwillingness to spend money adequately on the future of the nation during the past ten years has resulted, in spite of the emergency measures announced early in 1963, in a grave shortage of places in Training Colleges—and this at a time when there is a serious shortage of teachers. As a result, the Colleges are batting on a batsman's wicket and can select quite ruthlessly. The Training Colleges have always felt themselves to be the poor relations of the Universities. If they demand the same sort of entry qualifications as the Universities they feel they are putting themselves almost, or even quite, on a level with them. So, to the detriment of everyone, many colleges for women have been giving preference not to the candidates who have had the wide preparation which, as we have shown, is most needed for a teacher in a primary school, but to those who have had a narrow, specialized academic cramming in preparation for examination and whose values have inevitably been distorted thereby. Of course, other factors, such as personality and physique and the rest of it, are taken into consideration in selecting the candidates, but just how far the sanctification of the 'A' level has gone is shown by the following facts given by the Association of Teachers in Training Colleges and Departments of Education.

Unfortunately, the 7th report of the National Advisory Council on the Training and Supply of Teachers in Section 50 glories in this absurd system of preparing primary school teachers and states:

> One third of students following the three-year concurrent course now have two or more passes at the advanced level in the General Certificate of Education: another one-third have one such pass. We do not think it will be long before the great majority of students on such courses will possess academic qualifications on entry comparable with the minimum at present possessed by university students.

This would be a pleasing situation from the point of view of the dignity of the profession if it could be shown that studies

Admissions to Training Colleges September 1961/January 1962
for GENERAL three-year courses (i.e., not for Physical Education
or Domestic Science)

	Women approx.		Men approx.	
With 1 'A' level	1,982	(24%)	1,035	(26%)
„ 2 'A' levels	2,105	(26%)	923	(23%)
„ 3 „ „	991	(12%)	500	(13%)
„ more than 3 'A' levels	59	(1%)	43	(1%)
	5,137	(62%)	2,501	(62%)
With 5 'O' levels	507	(6%)	362	(9%)
„ 6 „ „	784	(10%)	356	(9%)
„ 7 „ „	672	(8%)	276	(7%)
„ more than 7 'O' levels	724	(9%)	266	(7%)
	2,687	(33%)	1,260	(32%)

pursued for 'A' level not only helped to develop the future teacher as a person but also were of some value to her or to him as a future teacher in a primary school. To test the latter point one has only to look through any of the published collections of 'A' level examination papers. Except in Biology, Geography and those aspects of modern language studies which are concerned with the living language, there is little indeed. For who would claim that 'A' level studies have helped the future teacher to develop as a person, have helped him or her to understand the forces which are shaping the world of tomorrow, or have given the student broad interests, wide sympathies and enjoyment of many aspects of the creative arts?

It is all too true that when those of us who have become professional academics look at 'A' level questions we find most of them fascinating. We would like to have hours to consider all the issues they raise. 'What are some of Voltaire's views on religion, as shown in the *Lettres sur les Anglais*?' 'Conflict between Church and State is healthier for both than the absorption of one by the other. Discuss.' 'How far is it true that Septimius Severus' work was solely destructive?' 'What influence did Great Britain's relations with other European states have on her policies in Africa up to 1914?' 'What historical significance has More's Utopia?' 'Discuss the role played by either (i) Churchmen or (ii) the common people in at least two of Shakespeare's Histories.' 'By means of a close critical analysis of the structure of any one novel (without merely retelling the whole story) discuss Dickens's powers of novel-construction.' 'To what extent does Rossetti's interest in the Middle Ages contribute to the success of his poetry?'

These questions, taken by turning at random the pages of the bound book of 1961 'A' level papers of one of the examining Boards, are all good questions either for very able young people with a flair for book study, or for adults. But I look forward to the time when a much larger proportion of adults than today will find great satisfaction in study and reflection, and I believe that topics of this kind, except for the gifted, are best held back till after school life. For those who are to proceed to the University they are, no doubt, necessary training, though one wonders whether they would not have been more suitable for university years. But for the majority of young men and women who want to teach children under 12, or less bright children between 12 and 15, these are difficult studies, absorbing an undue amount of energy and time and so limiting the broad development of spontaneous interests and creative skills. Of course it can be argued that 'A' level subjects, in their depth, train one how to study and teach the true meaning of intellectual discipline. But the myth of the 'transfer of training' has been exploded for a long time now and to imply that Grammar School teachers cannot give their pupils intellectual discipline without an 'A' level examination at the end of a course is an insult to graduate teachers. No; there is no sound reason for making all Sixth Form pupils jump through the same hoop: there should be different courses related to different lines of true development and one of these courses should have specially in mind the future teacher in primary schools and in lower classes in Secondary Modern Schools and many kinds of social worker.

By using this utterly false measuring rod the Training Colleges are doing great harm not only to the children who will later be taught by those selected for training as teachers, but also to the Grammar Schools today, particularly to the Grammar Schools for girls. It is less unreasonable, though it is still not good, for young men candidates for Training Colleges to be encouraged to take two 'A' level subjects, because many of them, even if they have to begin in primary schools, under Ministry pressure, will later teach in secondary schools. In these schools some measure of subject specialization, except for the teachers of 'C' streams and below, is bound to be necessary. And, in general, in my opinion, they should be encouraged to seek the secondary field just because, by and large, women are far better in teaching children in primary schools than men are. Nature provided them with a degree of patience and sympathy and kindliness and understanding with regard to these little ones that we do badly to ignore and to waste. As has already been urged, we should do all in our power, financially and by administrative arrangement, to keep all levels of the teaching profession attractive to women; indeed to make it more attractive than many other fields of life in which men can do equally well but in which women are employed because they can be paid less.

In particular, everything possible should be done to keep the primary schools mainly in the hands of women teachers and to see to it that there are enough of them to keep all our primary classes small—at any rate with thirty-five pupils as a maximum which must never be exceeded without special permission by the Ministry after special investigation by Her Majesty's Inspectors.

The Minister is content to hope that 'by 1975 the gap between teacher supply and demand would be cut to 21,000

11

if classes were to be cut to forty in primary schools and thirty in secondary schools'.[4] Even to achieve this, on present lines, will be difficult.

For these reasons we need to consider again the effect of the academic Grand National which has to be attempted by every young woman who would like to be a teacher, whether of 15 year olds or of 5 year olds in the infant school. Here are the figures regarding the proportion of Training College entrants who were accepted in 1954, 1955 and 1959 and who had had most, or all, of their schooling in Secondary Modern Schools:

1954/5	Men	150 out of 2,577	5·6% of total entries
	Women	138 ,, 8,092	2·0% ,,
1955/6	Men	111 ,, 2,545	4·4% ,,
	Women	140 ,, 8,153	2·0% ,,
1959/60	Men	140 ,, 4,102	3·6% ,,
	Women	174 ,, 9,606	1·8% ,,

The figures for the same categories in 1960/1 were not available, but the Ministry of Education has supplied those for 1961/2:

| 1961/2 | Men | 260 out of 5,739 | 4·5% of total entries |
| | Women | 232 ,, 12,061 | 1·9% ,, |

As about two-thirds of all boys and girls at present are educated in Secondary Modern Schools, this means that for two-thirds of the girls in the country the teaching profession is almost completely ruled out. Less than one in fifty of such girls at present get admitted into Teacher Training Colleges. Yet a much higher proportion than that must have not only the right personal qualities for handling children between the ages of 5 and 7 years, but also adequate intelligence to learn what they should know about such children and how to provide them with those play activities and foreshadowing of study which rightly constitute the curriculum of the infant school.

Clearly a very grave injustice is being done to the nation as a whole and to many thousands of adolescent girls who would make splendid teachers of the toddlers in our primary

schools. What is more, if the primary schools are to be adequately staffed we shall need many of these young women. It is
true that there are an inadequate number of places in Training
Colleges, by several thousand, for the number of young people
who apply with Grammar School background; but, surely,
as a matter of social justice, we must so extend our emergency
measures—or build so many new Training Colleges—that
suitable girls from Secondary Modern Schools *can* be given the
opportunity to become teachers.

I have already argued that reduction of the age of entry to
17 years would rescue young men and women in Grammar
Schools from the toils of a destructive period of 'A' level
study; indeed, so far as acceptance for training as a primary
school teacher is concerned, I would regard 'A' level results
as being almost a disqualification for admission, unless the
applicant could compensate by very fine personal qualities
and wide outlook. What the removal of 'A' level criterion
would also do is to open the doors of Training Colleges to
young women from Secondary Modern schools, for, as we have
seen, at present they are virtually excluded.

There is still one further argument in favour of the reduction
of the age of admission to three-year courses at Teacher
Training Colleges to 17 years. It is that for entry to a three-year
course for the profession of nursing the age has long been 17
years, although one would have thought that greater maturity
was required in the initial stages of this training than in the
initial stages of studies at a Teacher Training College.

Nevertheless, far from there being any desire to raise the
age of entry for training for nursing, there has been a move to
lower it.

Miss M. Henry, Registrar of the General Nursing Council
of England and Wales, at the annual conference of the Association of Hospital Management Committees in 1962 advocated
an earlier age of admission. She stressed the greater maturity
of young people today and added that adults arranging
training courses tended to look backwards to the school-
leaving age of the entrant, instead of forward to the early

age at which, today, they would marry. She emphasized, as we have tried to do here, that the whole picture of life for young people has changed and that we should adjust our regulations to meet these changes.[7]

For the health and happiness of society it is essential to give young people a chance to contribute to the welfare of the community as soon as they are ready for it. We have never hesitated to do this in times of war, when the term for Sixth Form schoolboys of 17 years changes overnight to 'Men' on government papers to Headmasters. We have therefore no excuse for trying to hold back our young men and women when there is vital work of a peaceful nature to be done. The contribution of such young people to Overseas Voluntary Service is an example of their capacities. Training College recognition of maturity among 17-year-olds might well be an encouragement to young people in other fields of life and do something to relieve the 'malaise of adolescents' to which Professor G. M. Carstairs thought it necessary to devote one of the Reith Lectures of 1962.

The return of married women teachers to the classroom

Reference has already been made not only to the richer contribution to the education of children that can be made by women who have had some experience with children of their own, but also to the very great *need* of such help in the schools. This assistance is absolutely essential if ever we are to be able to bring down the size of the classes to a maximum of thirty pupils.

In 1962 the report 'Investment for National Survival', produced by a committee presided over by Sir Charles Morris, then Vice Chancellor of the University of Leeds, stated that 95,000 additional teachers are needed by 1970 and that recruitment must now be raised to something between 30,000 and 35,000 per annum so as to allow for retirement and 'wastage'. The present output from Training Colleges is about 17,000 a year, and from University Departments of Education about 3,400 a year and recruitment of untrained graduates somewhat less. The present total from all sources is thus something less than 24,000 per annum. But total wastage, including retirement, is so high that this scale of recruitment of new teachers barely increases the total teaching force by 6,000 a year.

Hence there is a great need of what the Ministry of Education call 'married women returners' to whom we might give the rather more attractive title of 'released mothers'. But, according to the 1962 prediction of the National Advisory Council on the Recruitment and Training of Teachers, only 2,500 qualified non-graduate women can be expected to return each year to full-time teaching service in the years 1967–70.[8]

I would not dispute these figures. But I am of the opinion that many more married women who were formerly teachers would be prepared to return to the classroom if the conditions of their employment were made more attractive.

I believe that there are at present two strong dis-incentives to return to the classroom. The first is the pressure too often put upon them to take up full-time work when what they would really welcome—and do best—is part-time work. The second is the low salary, associated with the low tax-free earnings which the Chancellor of the Exchequer allows to married women.

The pressure upon 'married women returners' to teach full-time

The pressure upon married women to turn their backs upon their home and children all day shows itself first in the paucity of posts for which the advertisements state that part-time assistance will be considered.

This pressure arises from two sources—persistence of custom and difficulty with the timetable. Because at present in England and Wales even infant schools are whole-day schools for the children, the teachers have always been required to teach during the whole day. Removal of the pressure upon parents to send children to infant schools for the whole day, as suggested in Chapter 4, would at once make possible and encourage the employment of part-time teachers in primary schools.

Another incentive to schools to accept part-time teachers will arise from the introduction of the teaching of a modern language into all primary schools (see p. 65). For a number of years few of the present full-time class teachers will themselves be able to tackle this work properly. So it will be necessary, as at York and elsewhere, to bring in other teachers specially trained for the job. These could well be specially prepared 'released mothers' working part-time, for three good reasons. Firstly, even if the suggestions of Chapter 4 regarding part-time schooling of 'infants' come, by force of circumstances, to be adopted, the children who will learn a foreign language will be attending school full time and it would be unsettling for them to have part-time class teachers or a different class teacher in mornings and afternoons. But no such argument applies against having a language teacher for one lesson a morning. Secondly, mothers who, consciously or unconsciously, have taught their own little ones to speak English are likely to be more intuitively understanding in learning how to teach another tongue by the same 'direct' method. Thirdly, four or five lessons per day of 'direct' method teaching of language to little children is likely to be as much as anyone can do without loss of efficiency as the day goes on.

There has been even more reluctance in secondary schools of all types to employ part-time married women because of the very complicated timetable in such schools and because a part-time teacher does not expect to spend the whole day on the school premises with big gaps between her three or four teaching periods.

In the Grammar Schools for girls some good progress has been made largely as a result of the initiative of Miss Joyce Bishop, Headmistress of Godolphin and Latymer School, Hammersmith, who as early as 1947 stated, while serving on one of the advisory committees of the Ministry of Education, that the future staffing of girls' schools would have to depend on wives and mothers. Her initiative subsequently resulted in a survey to trace women graduate teachers who had married and to encourage them to return to teaching when they could properly do so. It was reported in January 1963 that on her own staff of forty women teachers Miss Bishop has fifteen who are married, nine of them part-time.

But the total number of women graduates between the ages of 29 and 60 years, whether new recruits or returning teachers, who took up full-time teaching service in the school year 1960/61 was 566.[9] As a result of publicity since then the figure may now have doubled, but, even so, as a contribution towards a recruitment of 30,000 teachers a year it is not very significant and ought to be increased.

But there is still, understandably, reluctance on the part of most Heads to undertake the extremely complicated task of building a timetable which is satisfactory both from the point of view of all the options and 'sets' and subject arrangements for the pupils and also to fit the convenience of part-time teachers. Even under the best circumstances the construction of a good timetable for a Grammar School (i.e., one that provides a wide range of alternatives for the pupils, the possibility of utilizing broadcast lessons, adequate practical periods for science, proper use of the games field, the scheduling of all mathematics lessons in the mornings, and so on) is a huge task. It is no wonder that most Heads, especially non-mathematical ones who do not enjoy weeks of wrestling with problems that often look insoluble, boggle at the idea of further complexities created by ladies who can be present only on certain half days.

Actually much more could be done to help Heads in timetable construction. The qualities required in a fine Head are sufficiently exacting that skill in constructing a timetable should not be an additional gift to be looked for or expected. Local Education Authorities could pay specialists, outside the school, to do the job for the Head, who should be required to submit only the list of lessons to be given by each member of the staff, the fixed points with regard to use of rooms and the desiderata in other matters. Retired Heads or other retired teachers who enjoy constructing timetables might be paid to do the job and electronic equipment could help. In any event, the maximum use of part-time 'released mothers' ought not to be held up by our failure to defeat the opposition sturdily put up by the inanimate timetable.[10]

The salary of the 'married women returners'

The financial dis-incentive is one which, perhaps un-intentionally, deals a double blow to a possible returner: one blow to the handbag and the other to self-esteem. The latter blow—and indeed the former too—arises from the existing national ruling that although many types of experience, such as office work or journalism, may rank for increment on the Burnham Salary Scale for Teachers, experience in bearing and bringing up children does not. According to the Secretary of the Salaries and Superannuation Committee of the National Union of Teachers the situation is as follows:

(1) There is no provision in the current Burnham Report under which it is possible for a Local Education Authority to recognise for salary purposes experience in bringing up children.

(2) The Burnham Report provides that all experience in gainful employment after 18 years of age prior to recognition as a qualified teacher shall be recognised on the basis of one increment for each period of three years' experience. It is also possible for the Local Education Authority, at its discretion, to recognise any of this experience after 21 years of age, if deemed to be of special value to the teacher in the performance of his particular duties on the basis of one increment for each year.

(3) The Burnham Report also provides that gainful experience after 21 years of age which is undertaken after recognition as a qualified teacher may be recognised at the *Authority's discretion* on the basis of one increment for each year, if it is deemed of value to the teacher in the performance of his duties.[11]

Accordingly, a woman who is returning to the profession at the age of, say, 35 years, after having brought up three or four children to the stage when her youngest is 5 years of age, may well return to the classroom at a salary little above that of a beginner. This, of course, is fantastic and is part of the low valuation so unfortunately put upon homemaking in this country. Homemaking is always bound to be much more than merely the physical care of children. And the type of young woman who has been selected, on academic and personal grounds, as suitable for training as a teacher, is one who is likely to have made a very good home and whose children are almost bound to have been brought up better than the average child, since the mother had initially an interest in children (that is why she entered Training College) and she there learned a very great deal about children, including child psychology. After that time she has been able to apply the theories and watch the effects. Could any preparation for educating children be better than this?

The greatest shortage of teachers in this country, now and for twenty years ahead, is that of women teachers of little children. Surely the experience which a woman, already qualified as a teacher, gets in bringing up children to the age, say, of 5 years 'is deemed to be of value to the teacher in the performance of her duties'? Any other answer than an affirmative to this question would be preposterous. So all that has to be done is to persuade the Burnham Committee to remove from paragraph 3 on the previous page, the word 'gainful'—itself a horrid indication of the false values in our acquisitive society.

Need for refreshment of 'married women returners'

Of course, after ten or fifteen years away from the classroom the woman will inevitably be 'rusty' in a lot of her academic knowledge, out of date in geography and so on. This leads, then, to the second point, namely that 'brushing-up' courses, usually on a part-time basis so as not to affect home life adversely, should be available for such people. If things develop as they should we must expect such courses to be a regular part of the educational provision of every town. Courses of this nature are already being provided by University Institutes of Education wherever there is a demand. But at present the demand is small, as an annual total of 2,500 'returners' from the whole of England and Wales clearly indicates.

There is, however, every reason to believe that the demand

would rise rapidly if, as suggested earlier, increments were given on the Burnham Scale for family experience. Indeed, the surprising thing is that the enriching experience of bringing up children should have been so long unrecognized. Over one hundred years ago Herbert Spencer foresaw this point also when he wrote:

> It is a truth yet remaining to be recognised, that the last stage in the mental development of each man and woman is to be reached only through a proper discharge of the parental duties.[12]

And we might add, incidentally, that experience as fathers is, as a rule, so valuable to men teachers in softening their asperities and increasing their understanding of children and adolescents that they should be financially assisted, like lecturers in universities, by a children's allowance on their salary in addition to that provided by the State.

Released mothers in work ancillary to education

In the report on 'The Education and Training of Girls', produced in 1962 for the National Council of Social Service, is was stated that

> ... nowadays a married woman is free earlier in her life to take up work outside the home and has longer in which to pursue it . . . but the community has not been quick to recognise this, nor to organise employment in such a way that her abilities can be used to the full.[13]

This, of course, is a typically British under-statement, especially because it does not mention the fact that by virtue of her upbringing of children the woman has now higher qualification for many kinds of social work than she had when she ceased to be 'gainfully employed' and took to child-bearing.

We have already referred to the different attitude in France where the experience of 'released mothers' is sought in such activities as school doctors, 'assistantes sociales', school guidance counsellors and officers of 'colonies de vacances'. We must hope to see similar developments in England and Wales.

CHAPTER TWELVE

Adults and Life-long Education

AWAY back in the nineteenth century the Universities of Oxford and Cambridge, as a result no doubt of the concern of a few protagonists, developed the admirable system of Extra-Mural lectures and tutorial classes whereby some of the literary and philosophical subjects might be taught once per week, in certain parts of the country, to small groups of keen, intelligent people who sought this kind of learning.

Subsequently the Workers' Educational Association was founded in 1903 by Dr. Albert Mansbridge and the Extra-Mural Delegacies have for many decades worked closely with the Association to the immense advantage of all adults seeking non-vocational education.

The question which arises now, however, is whether the universities, as a whole, are playing a large enough part in promoting the concept of life-long education. Particularly apposite, perhaps, is the persistence of the words Extra-Mural, even though a few vacation courses have for many years taken place inside university buildings and have been staffed with regular university Professors and Lecturers. But, so far as Oxford and Cambridge Colleges are concerned, except for these few 'Extra-Mural' courses, the use of the College building during vacation is little more than a means of grappling with the increasing costs of upkeep and of labour and of providing permanent work for people who, naturally enough, would otherwise be unwilling to be employed as College servants at any level.

As for the modern universities, they, too, endeavour to reduce deficits on their residential halls by letting them during periods of vacation. But just as, at a lower level, school buildings often cannot be used in evenings as much as they might because the cleaning and caretaking problem remains unsolved, so many halls of residence cannot be made available for student groups in vacations because of domestic considerations such as the necessary release of married women to look after their children during school holidays.

If we cast our eyes further around the country we find that Teacher Training College buildings, too, are to a large extent, despite some efforts to let part of them some of the time, empty for long periods of vacation, especially in the summer. Were we to consider the boarding Public Schools of England and Wales we should find still more residential accommodation, with attractive playing fields and swimming baths, lying idle for weeks of August even though, of course, some measure of decoration and repair is generally taking place on some part of the premises.

University Summer Schools

If we look across the Atlantic in the summer vacation we find a very different situation. The university premises, in most cases, are still swarming with life. They are by no means as full as during term and certain refectories and residential halls are closed and receiving decoration and repair or being expanded. But for an absolute minimum of six weeks during the summer vacation a large part of the university 'plant' is providing opportunities of continued education to adults. They may be doctors, nurses, dentists, journalists, farmers, horticulturists, engineers of all sorts, scientists of every brand, technicians, research workers learning fresh techniques, teachers deepening their knowledge in the academic or professional fields, and also adults who for their own interests are taking courses in modern languages and civilizations, painting, sculpture, music, drama, studying anthropology, sociology, philosophy, economics or some other social science.

In addition, during the university vacation, there may be residential courses for organizations of young people, especially of the groups concerned with agriculture, horticulture and home-making. The result is to give, rightly or wrongly, these young people still further stimulus to obtain Higher Education themselves.

Whilst all the foregoing applies to Canada as well as to the United States, it is worth recording here the following statistical information regarding the extent to which the growth of Higher Education is envisaged in the U.S.A. in the next few decades.

According to *Higher Education* of February/March 1961, a publication of the U.S. Department of Health, Education and Welfare,

> Projections of population growth and college entrance rates indicate that approximately 6,006,600 students will attend higher education institutions in 1970 and that about 4,504,500 of this number will attend full time.

The June 1962 number of the same journal tells us that:

> Colleges and Universities expect to increase their instructional accommodations by 41.2 per cent and their residential accommodations by 51.3 per cent between fall 1961 and fall 1965.

A break-down showing the types of institutions attended in 1961 by the student body, in percentages, is given in the January/February, 1962, number of *Higher Education*. This is:

Type of Institution	Per cent of total enrolment
All institutions	100
Four-year institutions	86·6
Junior Colleges	13·4
Four-year institutions	
Universities	41·9
Liberal Arts Colleges	28·5
Independently organised professional schools	10·3
Technological schools	2·9
Theological, religious	1·1
Schools of art	0·5
Other professional	1·5

The term Higher Education, when applied to the U.S.A., includes, of course, all that in this country would be included not only in Universities and Training Colleges and Colleges of Advanced Technology, but also much that is taught in Schools of Art, Agricultural Colleges, and in the three upper levels of Technical Colleges. Nevertheless, if we add together all our figures under these heads, we are still unable to claim anything like so high a proportion of young people continuing to study. As for the situation in the U.S.S.R. and other Communist countries, the emphasis there on continued study for everyone, at least in the vocational field, is so strong and the provision of free correspondence courses provided by Institutes and Universities so widespread, that again our proportion of students is likely to be out-distanced. In France it is officially expected that the number of students in Higher Education will be 600,000 in 1970.[1] This figure includes many students of high level of studies who are in French institutions of technical education, so comparison should not be made with the university student population of England and Wales.

But it is well known, and unfortunately incontrovertible, that when all such aggregate figures as 600,000 have been broken down, so that comparison is made only between numbers of university students at comparable level, the proportion of such students per thousand of population is lower in England and Wales than in most countries of comparable standard of living.

Yet in many fields we have so long held a leading place that it would seem unfortunate to allow ourselves to sink well below the level of our possible achievements.

At any rate, it is quite unnecessary: we have both the talent and the expertise. All that we lack is the resolution to break away the fetters of custom that at present prevent us from using our educational resources to anything approaching full extent. A country which has now come down in the world, we insist on behaving like the gentry we once were. Our wealthy cousins may use their educational premises almost throughout the year: *our* premises must have a summer period of leisure to emphasize the way of life once associated with retired pukka sahibs, or so it might seem.

Re-arrangement of the academic year

The first thing to be done, if we are going to make economical use of our educational plant and resources, is to rearrange slightly the academic year of both the universities and the schools. The summer vacations of our schools and our universities and training colleges are a little too short to provide the maximum incentive for their planned utilization. At the same time there is every reason to doubt whether the present length of Christmas and Easter vacations is either necessary or justifiable. Most parents of school children find the Christmas holidays a week too long and would be glad to see it cut down. With nearly as good reason a week could be cut off the Easter holidays, especially now that so many schools have a week of holiday at Whitsun. So all schools could end at least two weeks earlier in July than at present. The ending would still not be as early as in Europe or the U.S.A., but it would have four immediate advantages.

Firstly, the longer summer holiday would encourage the establishment of permanent holiday camps for youngsters as in France and the U.S.S.R. notably.

Secondly, it would enable all the G.C.E. examinations to be finished at least two weeks earlier, permitting earlier publication of 'A' level results to the great relief of both the universities and their candidates for admission. It would be such an advantage to Teacher Training Colleges that the Secretary of the Association of Teachers in Colleges and Departments of Education in 1962 approached both the Secondary Schools Examination Council and the Vice-Chancellors' Committee asking if it were possible for the Advanced Level examinations of the General Certificate of Education to be held in the spring to alleviate some of the problems of selection for acceptance.

Thirdly, it would be of very great advantage to the national economy and the health and happiness of the nation in giving families with children a longer period during which to select a holiday by the seaside. The advantages to the seaside resorts and those who seek seasonal work there are obviously very great.

In June 1960 the British Travel and Holidays Association convened a conference on this subject in London. There were representatives not only of such organizations as the Industrial Welfare Society, the Holiday Fellowship, the British Hotels and Restaurants Association, which can be regarded as prejudiced bodies, but also of the National Union of Teachers, the Association of Headmistresses, the Oxford and Cambridge Schools Examination Board, the University of London Entrance and Schools Examination Council and the University of Cambridge Local Examinations Syndicate. Yet the following resolution was passed *nemine contradicente*:

> That school examinations should be concluded not later than the middle of May, and that consideration be given to the staggering of holidays on a regional basis.

The change was urged as far back as in 1947 when the Secondary Schools Examination Council[2] recommended:

> The examinations should be held at such a time as will enable the results (at any rate for those candidates who seek awards) to be communicated by August 1st. We anticipate that this is likely to involve starting the examinations in May.

Nevertheless they still start in June.

Fourthly, teachers would have a vacation long enough to enable them to settle down either to advancing their knowledge or to teaching in special summer courses, as will be outlined below. Again they could help to run a holiday camp for a month without having too little time afterwards for their own refreshment. Yet again they could have broadening experience, such as earning their travel costs and pocket money abroad by taking some productive work in Canada or the U.S.A. or even as close as Western Germany for the two months vacation.

In order to bring about the most satisfactory reorganization of the school year it might be necessary also to shorten slightly (by not more than a five-day week) the minimum total of days during which state-aided schools must be open. Especially in view of the fact that any child who wishes to stay on at school beyond the age of 15 may do so, any educational loss would be infinitesimal.

So far as the universities are concerned they would be encouraged by the extra two or three weeks of summer vacation to commence, on a limited scale at first, perhaps in three- or five-year rotation among themselves, a system of six-week Summer Schools on the American plan. Of course some people will cry out at once that this would lower the standard of university teaching, not only by taking time from the most important period of a lecturer's own research work or lecture preparation, but also in so fatiguing the lecturers that throughout the subsequent year their normal university work would not be up to par.

If most lecturers were to be engaged on Summer School work in most years then both objections would become valid. But the number of adult students who can get away from their job for such a Summer School course can never be more than a small proportion of the number of undergraduate students, and if the American practice were adopted in recruiting, as part of the 'Faculty' for Summer School work, retired professors, distinguished people from other walks of life, and staff from other universities, including universities overseas, there need be no fear of the primary work of the university being adversely affected. Also, many research workers in industry would leap at the opportunity to do a little teaching.

On the other hand wonderful opportunities would be provided for adults to bring themselves up to date in a wide range of fields of thought and of skill. Anyhow no one would suffer from the carefully planned introduction of University Summer Schools. Many thousands of people would gain in enriched lives, many hundreds of thousands would subsequently gain indirectly through greater skill or productivity of doctors, youth employment officers, social workers, technologists and

12

technicians, and many hundreds of university servants in halls of residence would gain in overtime pay or other extra earnings.

Reduced to its simplest terms the University Summer School is an attempt to ensure that no opportunity of making knowledge available to people who can benefit from it is wasted. Even from *a priori* reasoning, however, one would not expect any scheme having such an objective to bring disadvantages to many.

Among the people who would benefit most from University Summer Schools, teachers naturally form a prominent group, especially lecturers in Technical Colleges and Training Colleges, who wish rightly to keep themselves abreast of the latest developments of thought in their fields. Close on the lecturers' heels come the teachers in the upper forms of Grammar Schools and after them come teachers at every level.

So far as the professional studies of teachers are concerned—*e.g.*, developments in psychology of the various age groups or methods of teaching handicapped children of all kinds, a wide range of courses is provided every year by University Institutes of Education. But, with few exceptions,[3] little has been provided that would enable teachers to deepen their academic knowledge, and while few teachers have more than a $6\frac{1}{2}$ week summer vacation, two weeks of which must be earmarked for a family holiday, there is not much point in laying on a six-week course of serious study, or even a four-week course, for there would be few takers.

But if the school year were to be rearranged on the lines suggested the situation would be very different, especially if, as in the U.S.A., a series of vacation courses could build up residential qualifications for obtaining degrees either by examination or by thesis. Teacher enthusiasm for increased knowledge has always been high and today it is such that whenever courses adjusted to their possibilities and to their needs are provided either by University Institutes of Education or by the Ministry of Education or by Local Education Authorities they are almost always heavily over-subscribed.

The part-time training of untrained graduate teachers

There is yet a further important way in which University Summer Schools could be of immediate help to the nation—namely in the part-time training of untrained graduate teachers. For many years now everyone concerned with schools, from the Ministers of Education downwards, has been agreed that it is wrong that people should be allowed to teach children without their holding some form of qualification which has ensured (*a*) that they were considered, on grounds of character and personality and temperament, persons suited to have control of children; (*b*) that they have pursued some appropriate studies of child or adolescent psychology; (*c*) that they have had the opportunity of studying some of the methods which today are considered most appropriate for teaching children of a given age range or in a certain field of subjects.

Sir David Eccles, then Minister of Education, on March 18th, 1961, stated[4]

"I think we must now run up a warning flag that at a not too distant date we shall expect all newly qualifying teachers to have professional training."

For decades there have been, at almost every university, one-year post-graduate courses of preparation for teaching. Every year thousands of graduates seek admission to these courses and selection is made from those that apply. But no graduate is obliged to seek any preparation for teaching.

At present in this country, and in this country alone so far as I am aware, any possessor of a degree of any university of the United Kingdom is thereby, *ipso facto*, a qualified teacher and entitled to payment as such on the Burnham Scale. His degree may be fourth class[5] in anthropology, but if any Headmaster chooses to employ him he may teach Mathematics or French, or what you will, as a qualified teacher drawing graduate salary.

Naturally, there are many graduates who make splendid teachers without any training and it is possible that the anthropologist just hypothesized might well be one of them, especially if his anthropological studies had involved his living for months in a primitive community and studying their concepts of number and the development of language.

But it does not follow that this is so, and the unfenced schools need some protection from the graduates who, rejected by several University Departments of Education as unsuited for the profession, are able, owing to the appalling shortage of teachers, immediately to obtain a teaching post in a school which is in desperate straits for staff. Such a graduate does not, of course, disclose that he has been rejected, for there is at present no obligation on a graduate to take any form of training or vetting for teaching, not even a vacation course.

The Ministry is unwilling, during the years of teacher shortage that lie ahead, to make the post-graduate year of teacher training obligatory for three reasons:

(a) many people, especially young women who are willing to teach only for a year or two while awaiting marriage, would enter other forms of work instead;

(b) one year of teaching by some thousands of young men and women would be withdrawn from the public supply;

(c) the University Departments of Education, even with the Training Colleges which cater for graduates, would be unable to deal with the increased number of students until both their staffs and premises have been extended.

But if the universities had Summer Schools of six weeks duration it would be possible and convenient to demand that all graduates who took up teaching without training should be required to attend three consecutive Summer Schools. Meanwhile they would receive advice and discreet surveillance while teaching, and would be qualified—or failed—by their results, practical and theoretical, over this period of time. The period of theoretical studies would then approximate to that devoted to such studies during the normal post-graduate certificate courses in the universities. So, in the course of time so far as the schools aided or maintained by public funds are concerned, we could gradually obtain a professionally qualified corps of teachers.

The effect of University Summer Schools upon the nation at large

But, over and above all such gains, however important at the moment they may seem, would be the effect upon the nation as a whole of this willingness of universities in long vacations to allow quite considerable numbers of adults to widen and deepen their knowledge. In a community dedicated to lifelong learning this action would provide evidence of the dedication.

There is one corollary that needs to be stated. It is important that most of the advances in the frontiers of knowledge should be achieved by public organizations which are not committed to further the causes of private profit, but to make universally available the fruits of their researches. So we should envisage, especially in the scientific departments of the universities, more rapid expansion of research facilities, so that private enterprise should not wrench from the universities their position of pre-eminence in the field of intellectual advance. If this means steady increase in the academic staff of universities then this in itself will contribute to the possibility of expansion of Summer Schools and to the easing of a number of educational problems not only in this country, but especially in the developing countries of the Commonwealth and the training of the staffs of their universities.

The Teacher Training Colleges and the developing countries

This leads us to consider the special contribution which the Teacher Training Colleges can make to the world by using, like the universities, their 'plant' and some of their lecturers, past and present, during the long vacation of one year in every two or three. The report produced by an Anglo-American Commission under the Chairmanship of Sir Eric Ashby, Master of Clare College, Cambridge, on the needs of higher education in Nigeria[6] put forward the suggestion that, to help the training college lecturers and other teachers in Nigeria to improve their rather limited professional and, often, academic knowledge, teachers from the United Kingdom should be flown to Nigeria to conduct vacation courses there during the English long vacation. Despite the very unorthodox nature of this suggestion, far more akin to the ideas of a religious group than to any which one would associate with a government department, the British Minister of Education was induced to give the support of his Ministry and the first annual group of English teachers went out to Nigeria in 1961.

What had surprised many English Ministry of Education officials in London, however, was the overwhelming number of teachers who volunteered for this difficult job in a climate to which one cannot adjust very rapidly. The response was, of course, a tribute to the fine quality of men and women in the teaching profession. Though this scheme is still continuing, and there is also the scheme of the Commonwealth Teacher Bursars which brings some 400 experienced teachers to the United Kingdom for a year of specialized professional study, yet the development of Nigeria alone requires far more help to teachers than can be made available through all existing schemes. And it needs the help more quickly.

It is here that Training Colleges can play an extremely important part, namely by the provision of Summer Schools for Overseas Teachers, especially for teachers in primary schools. For in such schools, overseas, modern methods resulting in the development of individual initiative are seldom to be found. And, especially in Moslem parts, such ideas will need to be presented in a concentrated drive if they are going to have a chance to take root. If at any stage in the next two decades there were no longer to be a need for such vacation courses in Training Colleges for primary teachers from 'developing' countries in the Commonwealth, there are many other developing countries which could benefit. Training Colleges could, of course, also provide courses of great value for overseas secondary teachers, but the need of the primary teachers is the more urgent and it is in this field that the Training Colleges have absolutely unrivalled expertise, at least in the Commonwealth.

Finally, if this picture of educational institutions in the United Kingdom as hives of almost unceasing industry seems either too trans-Atlantic or too much to be borne, or both, I would refer to Sir Isaac Newton's First Law of Motion. This states that

> Every body continues in its state of rest or of uniform motion in a straight line, except in so far as it is compelled, by external, impressed force, to change that state.

This law seems applicable to human affairs as well as to the solid inanimate objects which Newton had in mind.

It is my belief that in educational matters we of the United Kingdom have continued too long 'in a state of rest or of uniform motion in a straight line' and that, as a consequence, we are suffering economically, socially and in ways less tangible but even more important in the field of values. I believe that if we do not choose, of our own volition, to change, then after many vicissitudes lasting perhaps a generation, we shall be compelled 'by external impressed forces'—probably economic —to 'change that state'.

And that would be both a tragedy and an absurdity. For if we stir ourselves—and our Government—out of our lethargy, and reform our education to meet the need of the changed conditions of life, we can continue to play a leading part in the advancement of human freedom and the development of the highest qualities of man.

References

CHAPTER 1. *What's Wrong: Schools and the Social Environment*
1. Toynbee, A. J. *Civilization on Trial*, p. 25. O.U.P. 1948.
2. The first R. H. Tawney Lecture. November 1962.
3. *Essays on Education*, 1859. Dent Everyman's Library, p. 25.
4. Acts 17, v. 30.
5. Condorcet, *The Progress of the Human Mind*, p. 182. Translation by June Barraclough, Weidenfeld & Nicolson, 1955.
6. Condorcet, *The Progress of the Human Mind*, p. 187.
7. Marrou, *Histoire de l'Education dans l'Antiquité*, p. 146. Edition due Seuil, 1935. Translation by the writer.
8. *Le Problème Scolaire*. L'Institut Pédagogique National.
9. *The Times*. July 6th, 1962.
10. Rousseau, J. J. *Emile*, p. 172. Translation by B. Foxley. Dent, London.

CHAPTER 2. *What's Wrong: The Bottom Stream in Secondary Education*
1. Professor E. Paul Torrance in 'Measurement and Development of the Creative Thinking Abilities', *Year Book of Education 1962*, p. 125. Evans Bros., London.
2. Guilford, J. P. 'Parameters and Categories of Talent', *Year Book of Education 1962*, p. 123. Evans Bros., London.
3. From a Ph.D. thesis, 'Psychological Aspects of the Change from School to Work', by Miss Cora Tenen, presented to the University of Manchester, April 1948.
4. Douglas and Blomfield. *Children under Five*, Allen & Unwin, 1958.
5. Secondary Education. Report of the Consultative Committee. H.M.S.O. 1938.
6. *Bacie Journal*, Vol. 13, No. 4, December 1959.

CHAPTER 3. *What's Wrong: The Methods of Shaping Educational Policy in England and Wales*
1. Report of The Central Advisory Council for Education (England), Vol. I. H.M.S.O. 1959.

Chapter 3 (*Continued*).

2. *Op. cit.*
3. *Arts and Science Sides in the Sixth Form.* A Report to the Gulbenkian Foundation. Oxford University Department of Education. 1960.
4. *The Advancement of Science*, Vol. XIX, No. 79, p. 237. September 1962.
5. Dobinson (Editor), *Education in a Changing World.* O.U.P. 1951.
6. This plan, sometimes slightly modified, is now being adopted by several other Local Education Authorities and was recommended for Western Nigeria by the Banjo Commission in 1961.
7. *The Times Educational Supplement*, December 7th, 1962, p. 761.
8. Jonas Orring, *Comprehensive School and Continuation Schools in Sweden.* The Swedish Department of Church and Education, Stockholm.

Chapter 4.   *Civilization, Education and the Family*
1. Glover, *War, Sadism and Peace*, p. 231. Allen & Unwin, London, 1947.
2. Adler, A. *The Practice and Theory of Individual Psychology*, Translated by P. Radin. Routledge and Kegan Paul, London, p. 9.
3. Plato, *The Republic*, p. 66. Translation by A. D. Lindsay. Dent, London.
4. Bowlby, J. *Maternal Care and Mental Health.* W.H.O., Geneva, 1951.
5. Erikson, F. *Symposium on The Healthy Personality*, p. 102. Editor Milton, J. E. Senn, New York, 1950.
6. Rousseau, J. J. *Emile*, p. 13. Translation by Barbara Foxley. Dent, London.
7. MacCalman M.D., D. R. 'Problems of Early Infancy' in *Researches and Studies*, No. 13, January 1956. University of Leeds Institute of Education.
8. For an attempt to copy 'colonies de vacances' see *The Times Educational Supplement*, August 24th, 1962.

Chapter 5.   *Nursery Schools and Infant Schools*
1. Rousseau, J. J. *Emile*, pp. 57–58. Translation by Barbara Foxley. Dent, London, 1957.

CHAPTER 5 (*Continued*)

2. Ulne, John. *The New Primary School Statute*, Swedish Board of Education, 1962.
3. *Hansard*, July 13th, 1961. House of Commons.
4. Burnet (Translation), *Aristotle on Education*. C.U.P. 1903.
5. Report of the Conference can be obtained from The Secretary, Reading University Institute of Education.

CHAPTER 6. *The Junior School*
1. *Statistics of Education 1961*, Part I. H.M.S.O.
2. *Op. cit.*
3. Nunn, T. Percy. *Education, its Data and First Principles*. Arnold, London, 1947.
4. *Norway's Schools in the Battle for Freedom*. Royal Norwegian Government's Information Office. 1942.
5. Hjelmtveit, Nils. *Education in Norway*, Royal Norwegian Information Service. 1946.
6. *The Primary School*, p. 93. H.M.S.O. 1931.
7. Rowe, A. W. *The Education of the Average Child*, Harrap, 1959.
8. Locke, J. *Some Thoughts concerning Education*, Section 162. C. J. Clay & Sons, London, 1889.
9. *Education*, January 5th, 1962.
10. Penfield, Wilder Graves and Roberts, Lamar. *Speech and Brain-mechanisms*. Princeton University Press, Princeton, New Jersey. 1959.
11. Report purchasable from UNESCO Institute, Hamburg 13, Feldbrunnernstrasse 70.
12. Since this was written the primary school pilot scheme in the teaching of French, sponsored jointly by the Nuffield Foundation and the Ministry of Education, has been announced. It will start in September 1964.

CHAPTER 7. *The Secondary School*
1. Düring, Ingemar. *The Swedish School Reform*, p. 16. Appelbergs, Uppsala, 1951.
2. Read, Herbert. *Education for Peace*, p. 23. Routledge, 1950.
3. Koelle, W. *The Year Book of Education 1962*. Evans Bros., London.
4. *Ibid.*
5. Düring, Ingemar. *The Swedish School Reform*. Appelbergs, Uppsala, 1951.

CHAPTER 7 *(Continued)*

6. See the letter of Canon C. H. C. Hopkins, Vicar of Pallion, Sunderland, to *The Times* on August 3rd, 1962.
7. *Curriculum and Examinations in Secondary Schools*. H.M.S.O. 1943. p. 2
8. *Op. cit.*, p. 2.
9. *Op. cit.*, p. 3.
10. *Plato's Republic*, Section 415, p. 114. Translation by Lindsay. Dent, London.
11. *Curriculum and Examinations in Secondary Schools*. H.M.S.O. 1943. p. 3.
12. *Op. cit.* p. 4.
13. *Report of the Secondary Schools Examination Council*. H.M.S.O. 1947.
14. *Arts and Science Studies in the Sixth Form*. Oxford University Department of Education.
15. Since this was written a scheme for sabbatical leave has been introduced by Oxfordshire Education Committee.
16. *Journal of the Royal Society of Arts*, p. 830. September 14th, 1956.

CHAPTER 8.   *New Aims and New Methods in Secondary Education*
1. *The Times*, Educational Supplement, July 20th, 1962.
2. Child (Ed.), *The Independent Progressive School*, 1962. Leighton Park.
3. *Guardian*, November 20th, 1962.
4. Chinese is taught in five lycees in France and is to be taught in a Grammar School in England from September 1963.
5. The Franco-German treaty signed since this was written contains important educational provisions.

CHAPTER 9.   *Technical Education for Adolescents and Day-Release*
1. See Lady Gertrude Williams, *Recruitment to Skilled Trades*. Routledge, 1957; and *Apprenticeship in Europe*. Chapman and Hall, 1963.
2. British Association for Commercial and Industrial Education.
3. See No. 1 above.
4. *Hansard.* November 7th, 1960. House of Commons.
5. Statement by Ministry of Education, July 1962. Reported in *The Times*, July 21st, 1962.

Chapter 9 (*Continued*)

6. Quoted from *A History of English Education*, p. 233. Barnard, U.L.P. 1961.
7. Dobinson, *Technical Training for the Unskilled.* Technology, April 1959.
8. *Education*, June 29th, 1962.

Chapter 10. *Higher and Further Education*
1. *Universities Quarterly*, June 1962.
2. Only a small number of places can be offered in the next few years by the newly-created universities.
3. *The Listener*, p. 752. November 8th, 1962.

Chapter 11. *The Training of Teachers for Primary Schools*
1. *The Demand and Supply of Teachers 1960–1980.* Seventh Report of the National Advisory Council on the Recruitment and Training of Teachers. H.M.S.O. 1962.
2. *The Future Pattern of the Education and Training of Teachers*, p. 5. Eighth Report of the National Advisory Council on the Recruitment and Training of Teachers. H.M.S.O. 1962.
3. Wilson, Percy. 'The Unity of Knowledge', *The Advancement of Science*, Vol. XIX, No. 79. September 1962.
4. *The Times*, January 18th, 1963.
5. The Association of Teachers in Training Colleges and Departments of Education. *in litt.*
6. The Ministry of Education. *in litt.*
7. *The Times*, June 9th, 1962.
8. *The Demand and Supply of Teachers 1960–1980*, p. 12. H.M.S.O. 1962. Since p. 156 was written the Ministry has announced its emergency plans for Training College expansion.
9. *Ibid.*, p. 16.
10. Since this was written it has been shown that a timetable for a school programme involving 26 classes, 36 masters and 35 periods can be produced by an Atlas-sized computer in 90 seconds. Programming of the data would take about 6 hours. 'The Teacher', April 12, 1963. p. 3.
11. National Union of Teachers. *in litt.*
12. Spencer, H. *Essays on Education*, p. 114. Dent, London.
13. *The Education and Training of Girls.* National Council of Social Service, 26 Bedford Square, London W.C.1. 1962.

CHAPTER 12. *Adults and Life-long Education*

1. *Le Problème Scolaire*. L'Institut Pédagogique National, Chapter I. Ref. No. 8.
2. *Examinations in Secondary Schools*. H.M.S.O. 1947.
3. Reading University Institute of Education has provided two-week vacation courses in Chemistry and Physics and Biology for several years.
4. Ministry of Education. Press Release.
5. A fourth class is still awarded at Oxford, but it is probably no worse than the Pass Degree given in some universities to students for an Honours Degree whose marks are too low for a Third Class.
6. *The Ashby Report on Post-School Certificate and Higher Education in Nigeria*, Department of Technical Co-operation. 1959.